Freeway

Allgemeine Ausgabe

Englisch für berufliche Schulen

Vocabulary Notebook

von
Sabina Piatzer

Ernst Klett Verlag
Stuttgart · Leipzig

Freeway Allgemeine Ausgabe

Englisch für berufliche Schulen

Vocabulary Notebook

von Sabina Piatzer

Werkübersicht:
Schülerbuch, 978-3-12-800041-1
Schülerbuch, Ausgabe Baden-Württemberg, 978-3-12-800055-7
Lehrerhandbuch, mit Lehrer-Service-DVD-ROM und 2 Audio-CDs, 978-3-12-800042-8
Workbook mit 1 Audio-CD, 978-3-12-800043-5
Workbook mit 1 Audio-CD, Ausgabe Baden-Württemberg, 978-3-12-800056-5
Vokabellernheft 978-3-12-800044-2
Freeway Online-Ergänzungen unter www.klett.de/online

1. Auflage 1 6 5 4 3 2 | 15 14 13 12 11

Projektleitung: Matthias Rupp
Redaktion: Redaktionsbüro Sabina Piatzer, Hannover
Herstellung: Angelika Lindner

Umschlaggestaltung: ya:design, Roman Triebelhorn, Stuttgart
Bildquellennachweis: COVER Corbis (Bilderbuch/Design Pics), Düsseldorf; DHBW, Stuttgart
Satz: Redaktionsbüro Sabina Piatzer, Hannover
Reproduktion: Ernst Klett Verlag GmbH, Stuttgart
Druck: Medienhaus Plump GmbH, Rheinbreitbach

Printed in Germany
ISBN 978-3-12-800044-2

9 783128 000442

Inhalt

Abkürzungen und Symbole

BE	britisches Englisch
AE	amerikanisches Englisch
e.g.	Anwendungsbeispiel
=	synonym
↔	opposite
→	word family
·	Wörter aus anderen Units des Lehrbuchs

Service im Internet

Unter den **Freeway Online-Links** finden Sie die Vokabeln des Vocabulary Notebook zum Download im MP3-Format. Gehen Sie einfach auf www.klett.de und geben Sie den Online-Link in das Suchfeld ein. Weitere Hinweise erhalten Sie auf Seite 88.

Vorwort

Vokabeln sind das Einmaleins der Sprache. Sie sind unbedingt notwendig, um Texte zu verstehen, Fragen zu beantworten, Essays zu schreiben, Übersetzungen anzufertigen und vor allem natürlich, um korrekt zu sprechen.

Dieses Heft bietet Ihnen die Möglichkeit, Wortschatz aus Ihrem Lehrwerk zu festigen und zu erweitern, um sich effizient auf Ihre Fachhochschulreife-Prüfung vorbereiten zu können.

Wissenschaftliche Forschungen haben gezeigt, dass man sich thematisch sortierten Wortschatz besser einprägen kann als einfache Vokabellisten. Zu den so genannten Mnemotechniken zählt das Strukturieren von Vokabular in Wortfeldern. Darunter versteht man Zusammenstellungen von Wörtern, Strukturen und Redewendungen unter einem bestimmten Oberbegriff. In Unit 1 finden Sie zum Beispiel Vokabular aus *Freeway* zu den Oberbegriffen *„At college"*, *„Information about people"* und *„Work"*.

Um Ihnen das Vokabellernen zu erleichtern, bietet Ihnen dieses Heft als Lerntraining Wortfelder zu wichtigen Themenbereichen aus dem gesamten Lehrbuch. In jeder Wortliste erscheinen Vokabeln aus der jeweiligen Unit sowie Wörter aus anderen Teilen des Lehrwerks, die mit einem Punkt (˙) gekennzeichnet sind, zum Beispiel ˙*to pass* auf Seite 5. Dann folgen abwechslungsreiche Aufgaben, in denen Sie das Vokabular festigen und im Kontext anwenden.

Als weiteren Service finden Sie *talking vocabulary* unter www.klett.de: Alle Wortfelder stehen Ihnen hier im MP3-Format zur Verfügung, damit Sie die Aussprache hören und üben können.

Ebenfalls über einen Online-Link – 800041-0040 – erhalten Sie die berufsspezifischen Vokabeln zu den Bereichen Wirtschaft, Technik und Sozialpädagogik.

Für die Erweiterung Ihres Wortschatzes und die Vorbereitung auf Ihre Prüfungen wünschen wir Ihnen viel Erfolg.

Ihr *Freeway*-Team

Unit 1

Young people in Europe

At college		
to attend	teilnehmen	= to take part
· to pass	bestehen	to be successful in an exam
· to fail	durchfallen, versagen	e.g. to fail in maths, to fail a test; → failure ↔ to pass
to achieve	erreichen	to reach an aim; → achievement
IT	Informationstechnik	Information Technology
social care	Sozialwissenschaft	e.g. Social care workers help people in need.
Science	Wissenschaft	Biology, Chemistry, Physics
Geography	Geographie	a subject in which you learn about different countries
project	Projekt, Vorhaben	e.g. an environmental project
presentation	Präsentation	a talk about a special topic; → presenter → to present
essay	Aufsatz	a short text by a student
· theoretical	theoretisch	→ theory ↔ practical
term	Trimester	in Britain, one of the three periods of time between the school holidays
National Diploma	2-jähriges Studium am College	e.g. National Diploma in sport
leaver	Schulabgänger(in)	a person who left school; → to leave
· curriculum	Lehrplan	subjects one studies at college
· tutor	Klassenlehrer(in), Betreuer(in)	a teacher who works with one student or a small group

= synonym ↔ opposite → word family

Online Link
800041-0001

Information about people		
country of origin	Herkunftsland	the country you were born in
nationality	Nationalität	→ national
˙citizenship	Staatsangehörigkeit, Nationalität	→ citizen
˙residence	Wohnsitz	→ to reside
˙marital status	Ehestand, Familienstand	if s.o. is married or single; → married, to get married
˙gender	Geschlecht	e.g. The gender of a girl is female.
adult	Erwachsene(r)	= grown-up; → adulthood → adult
˙adolescent	Jugendliche(r)	= young person, youngster
personality	Persönlichkeit	→ person
lifestyle	Lebensstil	the way you live your life
behaviour	Verhalten	→ to behave
attitude	Haltung	a feeling or an opinion about people or things
˙membership	Mitgliedschaft	→ member
˙convinced	überzeugt	→ conviction
˙religion	Religion, Glaube	→ religious
campaigning	Aktionen; Wahlkampf führen	→ campaign → to campaign
˙activist	Aktivist(in), jemand, der sich für etwas engagiert	→ activity → active
aim	Ziel	= goal, target
dislike	Abneigung	↔ like → to dislike
˙habit	Gewohnheit, Angewohnheit	s.th. a person does often or regularly
impression	Eindruck	→ to impress
identity	Identität	who a person really is
subculture	Subkultur	a culture within a culture; → subcultural
˙condition	Kondition, Zustand	e.g. the condition of being rich and independent

= synonym ↔ opposite → word family

Work		
workplace	Arbeitsplatz	→ work → worker → to work
full-time job	Vollzeitjob	↔ part-time job
placement	Praktikum	a job where you can get some work experience
apprenticeship	Ausbildung	→ apprentice
trainee	Praktikant(in), Auszubildende(r)	→ traineeship → training → to train
nine-to-five job	geregelter Arbeitstag	a job with regular working hours
sales talk	Verkaufsgespräch	a talk in which s.o. sells s.th.
to take orders	Bestellungen entgegen-nehmen	e.g. Waiters and waitresses take orders.
coordination	Koordination, Abstim-mung	→ to coordinate
colleague	Kollege/Kollegin	a person who works with you

Exercises

1 Read the clues and complete the grid.

1 A subject in which you study Biology, Chemistry, and Physics
2 When you work on a particular subject at college over a period of time, you do a …
3 If you don't pass a test or an exam, you …
4 A list of all the subjects people must study at school, at college or at university
5 In order be successful at college you have to … courses regularly.
6 A subject at school or college in which you learn about different countries
7 A short text written by a student, especially as part of the work for a course

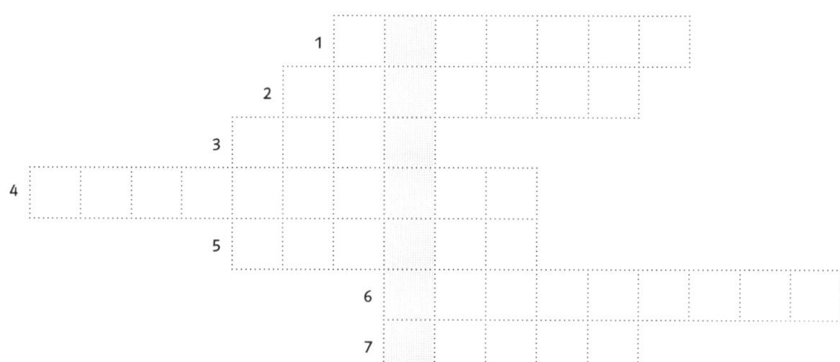

= synonym ↔ opposite → word family

2 **Word families: Fill in the corresponding nouns or verbs.**

Noun	Verb
impression	
	to reside
coordination	
	to fail
trainee	

Noun	Verb
leaver	
	to behave
presentation	
	to campaign
achievement	

3 **Complete these sentences with words from page 6.**

a) Your .... is the way you live your life.

b) A culture within a culture is called a ....

c) The country you were born in is your ....

d) Islam is a world ....

4 **Match the words on the left with the definitions on the right. Write down the right letters below.**

1	marital status	A	a strong opinion
2	aim	B	a feeling or an opinion about people or things
3	personality	C	belonging to an organization or group
4	conviction	D	something you want to achieve
5	gender	E	something a person does often or regularly
6	attitude	F	who or what you really are
7	habit	G	if a person is married or single
8	membership	H	the condition of being male or female
9	identity	I	all the important aspects of a person's character

1		2		3		4		5		6		7		8		9	

5 **Complete the statements by young people from Britain with these words.**

Geography	theoretical	orders	placement
social care	coordination	part-time job	National Diploma
apprenticeship	nine-to-five job	Information Technology	

Brendan, 20, from Newcastle: "I'm doing a ………………………………

in ……………………………… at college because I would like to help people.

At the moment I'm doing a ……………………………… in a youth club where I'm

getting some useful experience in working with adolescents. I don't mind working in the

evenings or at the weekend. I don't need a ………………………………."

Germaine, 19, from Bristol: "I've decided to study ………………………………

……………………………… because the computer industry offers lots of

interesting career chances. I like both ……………………………… and practical work, so

working with computers is just the right thing for me."

Damian, 21, from York: "Last year I started an ……………………………… as

a waiter. I'm working in a very busy restaurant and have to take lots of ……………………………….

In a restaurant, the kitchen staff and the waiters have to work together in an organized

way. Good ……………………………… is extremely important if you want to

have satisfied guests."

Rachel, 19, from Edinburgh: "I study ……………………………… and would like to work in

town planning later. To finance my flat I have a ………………………………

in a small boutique. I work there 15 hours a week."

Unit 2

Getting a job

Companies and company structures		
retailer	Einzelhändler(in)	→ retail → retailing → to retail
chain	Kette	e.g. a supermarket chain
superstore	großer Supermarkt	a very big shop where you can buy nearly everything
plant	Fabrikanlage	= factory
catering firm	Catering-Firma	a firm that delivers food and drink for parties and events
business field	Geschäftsbereich	e.g. banking or production
˙management	Management, Geschäftsführung	→ manager → to manage
personnel	Personal	the people who work in a company or an organization
headquarters	Zentrale, Stammsitz	the main offices of a company
˙branch	Zweigstelle, Zweig, Sektor	e.g. The company has opened branches in different countries.
manufacturing	Herstellung	→ manufacturer → to manufacture
research	Forschung	→ to research
housekeeping	Haushaltsführung, Raumpflege	→ housekeeper
˙turnover	Absatz, Umsatz	the total amount of goods or services sold by a company in a particular period of time
˙earnings	Einnahmen, Erträge	→ to earn
to expand	(sich) ausdehnen, expandieren	→ expansion → expansive

= synonym ↔ opposite → word family

Online Link
800041-0002

Applying for a job

application	Bewerbung	→ applicant → to apply
curriculum vitae	Lebenslauf	= CV = résumé
to type	tippen	e.g. You can find tips on the Internet on how to type an application.
qualification	Qualifikation	→ to qualify (for) → qualified
requirement	Anforderung	→ to require → requisite
candidate	Bewerber(in)	s.o. who is trying to get a job
advert	Anzeige	→ advertisement → to advertise
vacancy	Stellenangebot	e.g. a vacancy for a receptionist in a hotel; → vacant
permanent	dauerhaft	for a long time or forever
long-term	langfristig	e.g. long-term employment
challenge	Herausforderung	→ to challenge → challenging
rewarding	lohnend	→ reward → to reward
fluency	Sprachbeherrschung, Sprachgewandtheit	→ fluent
open-minded	aufgeschlossen, unvoreingenommen	= tolerant; → open-mindedness
active	aktiv	→ action → activity → to act out
reliable	zuverlässig	e.g. reliable workers; → reliability → to rely (on)
independent	unabhängig	→ independence → to depend
self-confidence	Selbstbewusstsein	→ self-confident
resilient	belastbar, stabil, robust	able to manage a problematic situation; → resilience
calm	ruhig	→ calmness ↔ nervous
discipline	Disziplin	→ to discipline → disciplined
essential	wichtig	= very important
with reference to	betreffend, bezüglich	→ reference → to refer
to enclose	beifügen	to send s.th. in the same envelope; → enclosure

= synonym ↔ opposite → word family

Food and drink		
sweet	Süßigkeit	e.g. chocolate and biscuits
confectionery	Süßwaren	sweets and chocolates
frozen	gefroren	e.g. Frozen food stays fresh for several months in a freezer. → freezer → to freeze
convenience food	Fertiggericht	food which is frozen or dried so it can be cooked easily
˙tinned	in Dosen, konserviert	= canned
loaf of bread	Brotlaib	e.g. Please go to the bakery and buy two loaves of bread.
˙salad	Salat	mixed raw vegetables
recipe	Rezept	instructions that tell you how to cook or bake s.th.
home-made	hausgemacht	e.g. home-made jam
˙groceries	Lebensmittel	→ grocer
˙cocoa	Kakao	Chocolate is made from cocoa.
˙cooking	Kochen	→ the cook → to cook

Exercises

1 Word families: Fill in the corresponding words.

Noun	Verb	Adjective
action		
	to challenge	
		rewarding
independence		
	to freeze	
		expansive
	to qualify (for)	
		requisite

= synonym ↔ opposite → word family

2 What do these words mean? Tick the right answer.

challenge:
a) a situation in which something becomes different ☐
b) something that is difficult and tests your ability and skill ☐
c) something that is dangerous and tests your ability to react fast ☐

manufacturing:
a) making things with your hands ☐
b) working in a factory ☐
c) producing things in large numbers ☐

fluency:
a) the ability to speak and write a foreign language easily, well and quickly ☐
b) permanent change in your life ☐
c) the ability to learn foreign languages very fast ☐

self-confidence:
a) the quality of people who think they can achieve more than others ☐
b) believing in yourself, your abilities and your knowledge ☐
c) the ability to do things on your own, not needing help from other people ☐

branch:
a) a local office, shop or factory that belongs to a company or an organization ☐
b) a small factory ☐
c) a new business field ☐

requirement:
a) presents you want from other people ☐
b) something that you must have if you want to do a certain thing ☐
c) the same as 'qualification' ☐

research:
a) the activity of going around and looking for things ☐
b) something you receive because you have worked hard ☐
c) a careful study of a subject, especially in order to find out new facts ☐

independence:
a) the ability to deal with stress ☐
b) the ability to live your life without help from other people ☐
c) the ability to manage a problematic situation ☐

3 **Read the text and work out the anagrams. Write down the correct words below. Then add the German translations.**

Tesco is the fourth-largest (1) LIRARTEE in the world. Since its foundation in 1932 the company has (2) DAXPEDEN steadily and has developed into the UK's largest supermarket (3) ICNAH. In 1968 Tesco opened its first (4) TEPURSEROS, a 40,000-square-foot store in Sussex. Nowadays you can find (5) HENSBARC selling all kinds of goods and services in over 4,800 locations worldwide. Each store is run by a (6) ENGANTAMME MATE like an individual business. With an annual (7) OTRUVREN of more than £60 billion, Tesco has remained highly successful even during the late-2000s recession. (8) QUERETSADHAR are in Cheshunt, UK.

(1) ....

(2) ....

(3) ....

(4) ....

(5) ....

(6) ....

(7) ....

(8) ....

4 **Replace the underlined words with words that mean the same.**

a) Your <u>curriculum vitae</u> has to be well-structured and up-to-date. ....

b) Mr Jones is <u>an open-minded person</u>. ....

c) A car company from Taiwan wants to open a <u>plant</u> in China. ....

d) Does <u>canned</u> food contain as many vitamins as fresh food? ....

5 Translate the words below and find them in the grid. Letters may overlap. One word has been given to help you get started. → ← ↓ ↑

1 Zuverlässigkeit
2 belastbar
3 Stellenangebot
4 dauerhaft
5 Lebenslauf
6 beigefügt
7 Anzeige
8 lohnend
9 Bewerbung
10 langfristig
11 erforderlich
12 unvoreingenommen
13 Bewerber(in)
14 qualifiziert
15 aktiv

O	R	E	W	A	R	D	I	N	G	N	U	H	K	Y	M	U	E	V
T	B	E	A	T	I	V	M	U	L	U	C	I	R	R	U	C	K	A
R	P	Y	C	T	J	S	M	R	E	T	G	N	O	L	I	W	S	C
U	T	N	E	N	A	M	R	E	P	Q	E	V	I	T	C	A	X	A
W	S	E	K	E	F	D	R	M	J	E	N	C	L	O	S	E	D	N
C	A	N	D	I	D	A	T	E	V	W	K	U	E	M	J	H	O	C
H	M	R	K	L	Y	G	H	R	E	L	I	A	B	I	L	I	T	Y
A	P	P	L	I	C	A	T	I	O	N	B	C	L	W	E	Q	U	F
M	G	Y	R	S	E	U	D	E	D	N	I	M	N	E	P	O	W	S
E	A	D	V	E	R	T	E	C	Y	Q	U	A	L	I	F	I	E	D
F	P	S	Y	R	L	E	T	I	S	I	U	Q	E	R	E	F	L	D

6 Complete the sentences with these words.

home-made groceries frozen sweets

recipe tinned cooking convenience food

a) .... is food designed for easy consumption.

b) You can prepare fast meals with .... and .... foods.

c) Experts say that if you eat fresh .... food and avoid eating too many ...., you won't have any weight problems.

d) However, shopping for ...., such as fruit, vegetables and dairy products, and doing the .... can be quite time-consuming.

e) Your soup was really delicious. Can I have the ....?

Unit 3

The youth market

Consumption		
consumer	Konsument(in), Verbraucher(in)	→ consumption → to consume
to purchase	kaufen	→ purchase
auction	Versteigerung	e.g. You can buy things cheaply in an auction.
bid	Gebot	e.g. winning bid; → to bid
payment	Bezahlung	→ to pay
to try on	anprobieren	to put on clothes in order to see if they fit
to exchange	umtauschen, austauschen	e.g. This CD doesn't work. I'd like to exchange it.
packaging	Verpackungsmaterial	→ to pack
to unpack	auspacken	↔ to pack
discount	Rabatt, Nachlass	= reduced price
˙ on offer	im Angebot	e.g. There is 50% off the shoes. They are on offer.
˙ inexpensive	preiswert, billig	= cheap; ↔ expensive
˙ must-have	etwas Unentbehrliches, ein Muss	e.g. this season's must-haves for any woman
˙ fashionable	modisch	→ fashion ↔ unfashionable
˙ trendy	modisch, trendig	→ trend
silver	Silber	e.g. This ring is made of silver.
˙ exclusive	exklusiv	e.g. Exclusive things are usually quite expensive.
˙ range	Angebot, Produkt-palette	→ to range

= synonym ↔ opposite → word family

Online Link
800041-0003

Trading and advertising		
advertiser	Inserent(in), Werbefachmann/-frau	→ advertising → advertisement → to advertise
agency	Agentur	e.g. advertising agency
promotion	Werbung, Promotion	→ to promote
marketing	Marketing	→ to market
merchandising	Verkaufsförderung, Merchandising, Vermarktung	e.g. In a merchandising campaign a football club sells products with the club's logo.
sponsoring	Sponsoring, Förderung, finanzielle Unterstützung	→ a sponsor → to sponsor
distribution	Vertrieb	→ to distribute
logo	Firmenemblem	a design or symbol that a company uses to advertise its products
· brand	Marke	e.g. The Levi's brand is known all over the world.
no-name product	Billigprodukt, Produkt ohne Markennamen	↔ branded product
target	Ziel	= aim, goal; → to target
commercial	Werbespot	During TV shows there are commercials for cars, coffee, mobiles …
slogan	Slogan, Werbespruch	a short phrase that a company uses to advertise its products
jingle	Jingle, kurze Tonfolge in der Werbung	a short melody which is easy to remember
flyer	Flugblatt	→ to fly
billboard	Plakatwand, Werbetafel	a board on which posters and adverts are displayed outdoors
trader	Händler(in)	→ trade → to trade
to be based	Geschäftssitz haben	e.g. The company is based in London.
· label	Etikett	→ to label
to create	schaffen	→ creativity → creative

= synonym ↔ opposite → word family

Mobile phones		
mobile phone	Mobiltelefon, Handy	= mobile, cellphone *(AE)*; → to phone s.o.
text message	Textmitteilung, SMS	SMS = short message service
premium rate number	Sonderrufnummer	telephone number for calls during which special services are provided
to delete	löschen	→ deletion
ringtone	Klingelton	e.g. My best friend has his favourite song as a ringtone on his mobile phone.
wallpaper	Hintergrundbild; Tapete	e.g. My boyfriend has my picture as a wallpaper on his mobile.
alert	Alarm	a signal that warns of a danger; → to alert
short code	Kurzwahlnummer	e.g. To get the latest football news send an SMS with 'foot-ball' to the short code 72404.
˙feature	Einrichtung, Eigen-schaft	= characteristic; e.g. features of mobile phones
˙battery	Batterie, Akku	a device that you put inside a clock, radio, mobile phone etc. which produces electricity
˙to reload	wieder aufladen	to load again, to top up; e.g. to reload a prepaid phone card
˙prepaid	vorausbezahlt	You must pay for it before you can use it
˙credit	Guthaben	e.g. I can't phone Emily because I've got no credit on my mobile.
˙user	Benutzer(in)	→ to use
˙instant	sofort	An instant message is s.th. you get right away.
˙operator	Betreiber(in)	→ operation → to operate; e.g. mobile phone operator
˙digital	digital	storing information as numbers or electronic signals

= synonym ↔ opposite → word family

Law and regulations		
right	Recht	e.g. Children don't have the right to drive cars. It's illegal.
regulation	Regel, Vorschrift	an official rule; → to regulate
contract	Vertrag	a legal agreement between two people or groups
to agree in a contract	einen Vertrag abschließen	to sign a contract
confirmation	Bestätigung	→ to confirm
cooling-off period	Widerspruchsfrist	the period during which a buyer can get his money back
scam	Betrug	a clever illegal plan to make money; → to scam
crime	Verbrechen, Kriminalität	e.g. to commit a serious crime, a high crime rate; → criminal
˙to prove	beweisen	to show that s.th. is true
˙evidence	Beweis, Beweismaterial	s.th. that makes s.th. clear or that proves s.th.; → evident
ban	Verbot	→ to ban
˙penalty	Strafe	= punishment
˙prohibition	Verbot	a law that makes s.th. illegal; → to prohibit
˙offender	Angreifer(in), Täter(in)	s.o. who has done s.th. wrong; → offence → to offend

Exercises

1 Word building: Write down the corresponding nouns. What do they all have in common? Are there any differences?

to prohibit .... to regulate ....

to distribute .... to delete ....

to promote .... to operate ....

= synonym ↔ opposite → word family

2 Find eight noun-verb pairs in the lists on pages 16 to 19 that have the same forms.

Noun	Verb

Noun	Verb

3 Use some words from exercise 2 to fill in the gaps.

a) Marketers use clever methods to .... children in commercials.

b) As kids have difficulties distinguishing between advertising and reality, parents' organizations call for a .... on all advertising aimed at children.

c) Mr Taylor lost a lot of money in an insurance ....

d) In case of fire you have to .... the fire brigade as quickly as possible.

e) Designer .... clothing is mostly bought by the upper-middle class.

f) Before you place a .... in an Internet auction, you should become familiar with the auction site and find out about its rules.

g) In a superstore you can find a huge .... of products.

h) The software company announced its $30 million .... of one of its major competitors.

4 Mark the word in each row that does not go with the others. Explain your choice.

a) marketing – distribution – trendy – consumption ....

b) text message – ringtone – user – wallpaper ....

c) scam – ban – penalty – prohibition ....

d) commercial – auction – jingle – advertisement ....

e) trader – consumer – flyer – advertiser ....

5 Read the clues and fill in the grid.

1 When something is on offer you can buy it at a …
2 A product that many people want to have
3 A person who buys something in order to use it on their own
4 The act of paying money for something
5 The same as 'cheap'
6 A white metal that is used for making coins, rings, knives and forks
7 Popular and trendy
8 Paper, plastic or other materials around products that are sold in shops

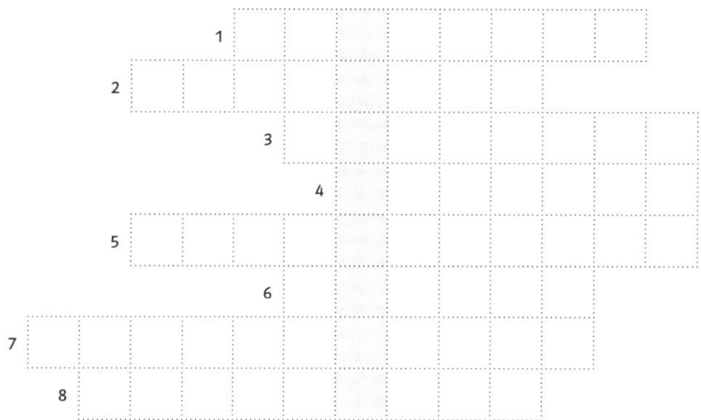

6 Complete the words.

a) Before a company starts to c…t…a br… it must identify the possible costumers so that p…m…t… of its products will be effective.

b) A unique business l…g… is essential for successful m…ch…d… .

c) Big companies often use sp…r… as a tool of m…t…g.

d) So-called n…-n…m…p…d…s are usually distinguished from b…d…d products, although most of them have a name, which is just lesser-known and not ad…e…t…ed.

e) B…b…ds can typically be found on the sides of busy roads and present large a…e…t…m…s, often with original s…o…s, to pedestrians and drivers.

7 Complete the sentences with these expressions.

premium-rate number | wallpapers | credit | battery | ringtones | prepaid | short codes | features | text messages

a) Young children don't need mobile phones with a lot of different ______.

b) Giving children ______ mobile phones is a good way to teach them how to be responsible with their ______.

c) A survey done in 2009 showed that over 50% of American teenagers send at least 50 ______ ______ per day.

d) A lot of young adults like to personalize their mobile phones by downloading ______ with complicated melodies or ______ with unusual images.

e) Oh no, my mobile says "Low ______" and I left my charger at home!

f) Before calling a ______ ______ find out how much you will be charged.

g) ______ are easier to read and remember than other phone numbers.

8 Match the sentence parts.

1. An offender is a person
2. If you agree in a contract
3. It is a basic human right
4. A penalty is
5. If you want to prove a crime
6. During a cooling-off period

a) a punishment for an action that is against the law.
b) a customer can return a product.
c) you need clear evidence.
d) who commits a crime.
e) to think and speak freely.
f) you sign it.

1. 2. 3. 4. 5. 6.

Unit 4

Media in our lives

Computers		
messaging service	Dienst zur Sofortversendung von Nachrichten	e.g. ICQ and Skype are instant messaging services.
icon	Icon, Bildschirmsymbol	e.g. menu icon, trash can icon
to click	klicken	→ click
to update	aktualisieren	→ update
button	Knopf, Taste	e.g. Press the left mouse button.
to download	herunterladen	→ download
file	Datei	e.g. Don't forget to save the file!
wireless	drahtlos	→ wire; WLAN = wireless local area network
programming language	Programmiersprache	→ program → programmer → to program
games console	Spielekonsole	an electronic device used to play video games
provider	Anbieter	→ provision → to provide
keypad	Tastatur	= keyboard
· search engine	Suchmaschine	It helps you to find information on the Internet; → to search
· domain	Domain	part of a website address
· TLD (top-level domain)	Bereich oberster Ebene	The last letters of an Internet address show its top-level domain, e.g. 'de' for Germany.
· to google	googeln	to search for information on the Internet using Google
· data	Daten	facts, items of information

= synonym ↔ opposite → word family

Online Link 800041-0004

Talking and writing		
conclusion	Schlussfolgerung	→ to conclude
to summarize	zusammenfassen	→ summary
to sum up	zusammenfassen	If you sum up what happens in a story, you explain it in a few sentences.
to comment	kommentieren, Stellung nehmen	to give one's opinion on s.th.; → comment
to propose	vorschlagen	→ proposal
report	Bericht	→ reporter → to report
analysis	Analyse	→ to analyze
to point out	hinweisen auf	If you point out a fact, you tell s.o. about it.
pros and cons	Argumente für und gegen etwas	= advantages and disadvantages
to suggest	vorschlagen	= to propose; → suggestion
context	Kontext, Zusammenhang	the text that comes before and after a particular text passage
Crime and justice		
to steal	stehlen	to take s.th. without permission and keep it
thief, pl. thieves	Dieb	→ theft
killing	Tötung	→ killer → to kill
murder	Mord	→ murderer → to murder
piracy	Piraterie, Raubkopieren	→ pirate
witness	Zeugin, Zeuge	→ to witness
illegal	illegal, gesetzeswidrig	↔ legal
responsible (for)	verantwortlich (für), haftbar	→ responsibility
prison	Gefängnis	a building where criminals must live as a punishment
court	Gericht	Before people are sent to prison, they have to appear in court.
judge	Richter	a person who decides in court

= synonym ↔ opposite → word family

1 Read the clues and fill in the crossword.

Across:

3 Items of information
5 The latest improvements to a computer programme
6 Not using wires
8 The same as 'keyboard'
10 A small object that you press to make a machine or computer work
11 Information that you store on your computer under a particular name
12 A language that makes computers work
13 A website that collects and organizes information from all over the Internet

Down:

1 An electronic device used to play video games
2 The highest level of domain names on the Internet
4 Sending a message over a computer network using software that immediately shows the message
7 A small symbol on a computer screen
9 A company that makes Internet services available to users, often a phone or cable company

2 **Word families: Fill in the corresponding nouns or verbs.**

Noun	Verb
search	
	to click
killing	
	to witness
comment	
	to conclude

Noun	Verb
	to summarize
download	
	to propose
report	
	to suggest
Google	

3 **Complete the sentences with these words.**

point out — summary — suggest — pros and cons — context — proposal — analysis — comment

a) A ______________ is an essay in which you first discuss some important ______________ of a statement or a thesis and then give your opinion.

b) You can easily understand new words and phrases if you look closely at the ______________.

c) A ______________ is a short text in which you present in your own words the most important aspects of a text that you have read.

d) In a cartoon ______________ you explain what the cartoonist wants to ______________.

e) If you are against the introduction of CCTV at this college, you have to be able to ______________ good alternatives.

f) A debate is a discussion in which you give reasons for and against a ______________.

4 Finish the definitions.

a) A judge is a person who ……………………………………

b) A murderer is a person who ……………………………………

c) A reporter is a person who ……………………………………

5 Read the text and work out the anagrams. Write down the correct words below. Then add the German translations.

The film and music industries say that (1) CRYPIA on the Internet is costing them billions of dollars. One in four Internet users admits to having (2) WENDODODAL films. This is an act of (3) NEGLASIT called copyright (4) FEHTT. (5) GLALILE copying of digital entertainment has become an immense problem all over the world. A lot of states now punish copyright (6) VITESHE with tough penalties. (7) TRUCSO have also convicted operators of so-called BitTorrent trackers, which are Internet services providing links to songs, films, video games and other material and helping users to download (8) SIFEL. Some of these people were sent to (9) SORNIP and had to pay damages to leading entertainment companies.

(1) …………………… ……………………

(2) …………………… ……………………

(3) …………………… ……………………

(4) …………………… ……………………

(5) …………………… ……………………

(6) …………………… ……………………

(7) …………………… ……………………

(8) …………………… ……………………

(9) …………………… ……………………

Unit 5

Social change

Work		
wage	Lohn	money that is paid for work
salary	Gehalt	money that is paid every month for work
profession	Beruf	e.g. the profession of teaching; → professional
commitment	Engagement, Verpflichtung, Bekenntnis	When you work towards s.th. you show your commitment to it.
opportunity	Gelegenheit	= chance; e.g. job opportunities
unpaid	unbezahlt	↔ paid
voluntary	freiwillig, ehrenamtlich	→ volunteer → to volunteer
labour	Arbeits-	= work
organizational	organisatorisch	→ organization → to organize
mechanical	mechanisch, technisch	→ mechanic
motivation	Motivation, Leistungsbereitschaft	→ to motivate → motivated
routine	Routine, Tagesablauf	regular tasks in a fixed order
task	Aufgabe	a piece of work that is difficult or that you don't enjoy doing
shift	(Arbeits-)Schicht	a period of work
function	Funktion, Aufgabe(nbereich)	= role, purpose, task; → to function → functional
demanding	anspruchsvoll	→ demand → to demand
conference	Konferenz	a meeting to discuss s.th.
to interact	interagieren, zusammenwirken	→ interaction → interactive
creative	kreativ, schöpferisch	→ creativity → to create

= synonym ↔ opposite → word family

Online Link
800041-0005

Women, partnership and family

missus	umgangssprachliche Anrede für eine Frau	→ Mrs
pregnancy	Schwangerschaft	→ pregnant
feminist	Feministin, Frauenrechtlerin	→ feminism
female	weiblich	↔ male
beauty	Schönheit	→ beautiful
contraception	Schwangerschaftsverhütung	→ contraceptive
engaged	verlobt	having agreed to marry s.o.; → engagement → to become engaged
· relationship	Beziehung	the way in which two people behave and feel towards each other
· partnership	Partnerschaft	a relationship between two people or also between firms, organizations etc.
affair	Affäre	a secret sexual relationship
condom	Kondom	You can have safer sex if you use a condom.
· impotence	Impotenz, Zeugungsunfähigkeit	→ impotent
· marriage	Heirat, Hochzeit	→ to marry → married
· wedding	Hochzeit	e.g. Paul and Jane really love each other. Their wedding is on Friday.
· honeymoon	Hochzeitsreise	journey after one's wedding
single parent	Alleinerziehende(r)	= lone parent
single mum	alleinerziehende Mutter	woman who is a single parent
· offspring	Nachwuchs, Nachkommen	= child, children
· grandchild	Enkelkind, Enkel(in)	→ grandson → granddaughter

= synonym ↔ opposite → word family

Society and social issues		
society	Gesellschaft	→ social
˙anti-social	asozial, antisozial	hurting other people
western	westlich	→ west
situation	Situation	what is happening at the moment
environment	Umgebung, Umfeld	the people and things around you
community	Gemeinde, Gemeinschaft	e.g. Our village is a small community.
norm	Norm, Regel	a way of behaving that people expect from you
tradition	Tradition	→ traditional
conventional	konventionell, normal	= normal, typical; → convention
poverty	Armut	→ poor
˙benefit	Sozialhilfe, Rente	e.g. They don't have jobs and get benefits from the state.
˙welfare	Sozialhilfe, Wohlfahrt	money provided by the state to people who have no job
˙homelessness	Obdachlosigkeit	not having a home
˙violence	Gewalt	→ to violate → violent
˙racism	Rassismus	→ racist
˙bullying	Mobbing, Schikanieren	being aggressive towards s.o. weaker
˙binge drinking	Besäufnis, Komasaufen	the consumption of large quantities of alcohol within a short period of time
˙deprived	sozial benachteiligt	→ deprivation
˙to hang around	herumhängen	to wait and not do very much
˙failure	Versagen	→ to fail
handicapped	behindert, benachteiligt	= disabled → handicap
˙childcare	Kinderbetreuung	→ child carer
˙rundown	abgewirtschaftet, verwahrlost	e.g. The building was empty and completely rundown.
focus	Blickpunkt, Mittelpunkt, Fokus	a central point of attention, e.g. focus on childcare

= synonym ↔ opposite → word family

School		
comprehensive school	Gesamtschule	schools for people from 11 to 16 or 18 years old
special needs	Sonderschul-	Special needs teachers can help pupils with learning difficulties.
nursery school	Vorschule	a school for children between three and five years of age
primary school	Grundschule	the first school you go to
secondary school	weiterführende Schule	high school
head teacher *(BE)*	Schulleiter(in)	principal *(AE)*
coaching	Nachhilfeunterricht, Coaching	special classes, often private, given to one person or to a small group
certificate	Zeugnis, Urkunde, Bescheinigung, Zertifikat	When you pass an exam, you will get a certificate.
GCSE	Prüfung zum Abschluss der Sekundarstufe	General Certificate of Secondary Education
campus	Campus, (Hoch-) Schulgelände	area of land with the buildings of a university or school
yard	Hof	an area outside a building
corridor	Gang, Flur, Korridor	e.g. The students walked down the corridor to their classroom.

Exercises

1 Word building: Add the right endings to the nouns.

-ion -ary -ship -ment -ness -ity -ism

relation	funct	sal ....
opportun	environ	homeless ....
interact	rac	contracept ....
femin	creativ	commit ....

= synonym ↔ opposite → word family

2 **Word families: Fill in the corresponding nouns or adjectives. Then use a dictionary to add the German translation of each word.**

Noun	**Adjective**
violence – *Gewalt*	
	voluntary –
society –	
	demanding –
marriage –	
	beautiful –
handicap –	
	conventional –
interaction –	
	creative –
racism –	
	functional –

3 **Collocations: Combine the verbs from the left box with the phrases from the right box. Write down all the possible combinations.**

to be • to get • to have • to become	a conference • pregnant • married • a relationship • engaged • a small wage • benefits • a handicap • a high salary • an affair

Now explain why 'become' is a false friend.

4 Complete the sentences with these words.

shift motivation commitment (2x) organizational conference
opportunities organized professions interact labour
tasks unpaid routine mechanical

a) Medicine, nursing, law, teaching and engineering are ______________.

b) Voluntary work is a form of social ______________ and it is ______________.

c) In a basic ______________ skills seminar you learn how to use different tools.

d) Why don't Western European governments do more to keep foreign students in their ______________ markets?

e) The job ______________ in health care management will be very good in the next few years.

f) ______________ work is physically demanding, especially if you have to work at night.

g) Jason's daily ______________ is strictly ______________ around his studies.

h) People who are satisfied with their jobs have a high ______________ to work and be successful, whereas people who have to work under difficult conditions often do not show much ______________ when performing their ______________.

i) Studies also show that people who ______________ well at their workplace are usually able to achieve their individual and ______________ goals.

j) Last weekend representatives from all continents attended a ______________ on working conditions for women in different parts of the world.

5 Complete the words. You can find all of them on page 29.

a) C_n__a__p___n helps people to prevent unwanted __r__n__c__s.

b) Using c__d__s immensely lowers the risk of being infected with HIV.

c) Since the 19th century f__i___ activists have fought for women's rights.

d) No one has counted yet all the many poems on __e__a__b___y.

e) In western societies nowadays not many couples get e_g___ before they m___y.

f) However, a lot of them want to have a formal, pompous w_d___ and at least one week of _o__m__.

g) Researchers found out that, contrary to popular belief, men suffer more than women when a r_l___s__ ends.

h) Couples often break up because they have different ideas of __r_n___ip.

i) The daily lives of s__g__p___s can be very stressful.

6 Match the words on the left with the definitions on the right.

1	tradition	A	all the people living in one place who are regarded as a group
2	failure	B	a way of behaving that people expect from you
3	community	C	disadvantaged in some way
4	poverty	D	not taken care of and therefore in a very bad condition
5	violence	E	something that people in a society have done for a long time
6	rundown	F	a central point of attention
7	focus	G	lack of success
8	deprived	H	hurting or even killing others
9	norm	I	the condition of being poor

1	2	3	4	5	6	7	8	9

7 Translate the clues and write the English words in the crossword.

Across:
4 Kinderbetreuung
7 Obdachlosigkeit
8 Gesellschaft
9 Rassismus
10 Mobbing

Down:
1 Umfeld
2 Komasaufen
3 Sozialhilfe
5 antisozial
6 Wohlfahrt

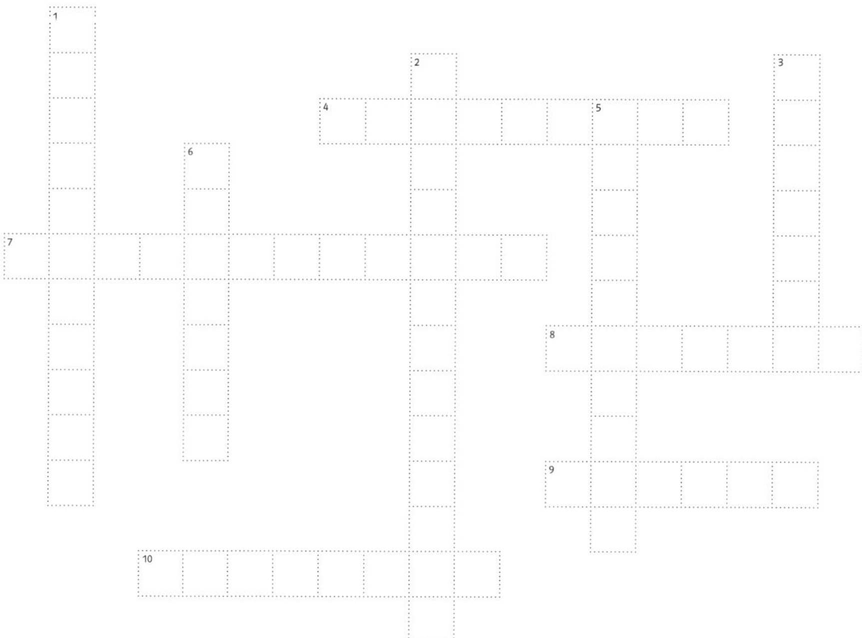

8 Complete the sentences with expressions from page 31.

a) The first school you go to is ______ ______ and after that you go to ______ ______.

b) About 90 % of British pupils attend ______ ______, which are similar to German *Gesamtschulen*.

c) If you have problems in maths, perhaps ______ will help you.

d) Common ______ ______ include disabilities and challenges with learning.

Unit 6

Ecology

Nature		
natural	natürlich	→ nature ↔ unnatural
rainfall	Niederschlag, Regen	rain + fall = rainfall
· rainforest	Regenwald	rain + forest = rainforest
season	Jahreszeit, Saison	e.g. Summer is the warmest season.
resource	Ressource, Bodenschatz, Rohstoff	e.g. It is important not to waste the world's natural resources.
to run out	ablaufen, auslaufen, zu Ende gehen	e.g. Will the earth run out of resources by 2050?
crystal	Kristall	a mineral (e.g. diamond) that has a regular shape
gas	Gas, Benzin	any substance like air; gas *(AE)* = petrol *(BE)*
solar	Sonnen-, Solar-	e.g. solar energy; → sun
nuclear	nuklear, Atom-	= atomic; e.g. nuclear waste
wave	Welle	When there is a storm at sea there are huge waves.
algae pl.	Algen, Tang	plants that live in the water
· desert	Wüste	It doesn't rain often in the desert.
· countryside	Landschaft, Land	e.g. Britain's beautiful countryside, living in the countryside
· wilderness	Wildnis	→ wild
· wildlife	Tierwelt (in freier Wildbahn)	all animals that don't live in zoos, people's homes or on farms
· unspoiled	unberührt, unbeschädigt	= undamaged, intact

= synonym ↔ opposite → word family

Online Link
800041-0006

Environment		
· environmental	Umwelt-	e.g. environmental organization
ecology	Ökologie	→ ecological
eco-	Öko-	Our car is eco-friendly.
to recycle	recyceln, wiederverwerten	→ recycling → to recycle → recyclable
global	global	relating to the whole world
warming	Erwärmung	→ warm
fossil fuel	fossiler Brennstoff	Coal and oil are fossil fuels.
to emit	emittieren, ausstoßen	= to give out or send out; → emission
carbon dioxide	Kohlendioxyd, CO_2	You get CO_2 gases when you burn coal or wood.
increasing	zunehmend, steigend, wachsend	→ increase → to increase ↔ decreasing
conservation	Erhaltung, Schutz	→ to conserve
to save	sparen	e.g. to save resources
organic	biologisch angebaut, organisch	= natural
water-related disease	Krankheit, die durch (unsauberes) Wasser verursacht wird	e.g. In Africa you find many water-related diseases.
disaster	Katastrophe, Desaster	a very bad accident
catastrophe	Katastrophe	an extremely terrible disaster
overfishing	Überfischung	→ fishing → fish
to harm	schaden, verletzen	→ harmful
low-flush toilet	Toilette mit geringem Wasserverbrauch	e.g. You can save water by using low-flush toilets.
sustainable	nachhaltig	e.g. sustainable development
· to exploit	verwerten, ausbeuten	→ exploitation
· toxic	giftig	= poisonous
· biofuel	Biotreibstoff	bio(logical) + fuel = biofuel
· bioreserve	(Bio-)Reservat	area where nature is protected
· sewage	Abwasser	dirty waste water

= synonym ↔ opposite → word family

Dealing with problems/commitment		
worry	Sorge, Ärger	→ to worry → worried
concern	Bedenken, Sorge, Anliegen	a feeling of worry; → concerning → concerned
negative	negativ	= bad, harmful; ↔ positive
to identify (with)	herausfinden, (sich) identifizieren (mit)	→ identification
issue	Angelegenheit, Problem	= topic
aspect	Aspekt, Gesichtspunkt	e.g. This aspect of the problem is the most important.
complex	komplex, vielfältig, kompliziert	consisting of many parts; e.g. a complex problem; ↔ simple
conscience	Gewissen, Bewusstsein	sense of what is right and wrong
responsibility	Verantwortung	→ responsible
to aim	anstreben, zielen	→ aim
to contribute	beitragen	→ contribution
to provide s.o. with	jmdn. versorgen mit	e.g. to provide people with water
assistance	Hilfe	→ assistant → to assist
to benefit (from)	Nutzen ziehen (aus), profitieren (von)	e.g. to benefit from aid projects
non-profit	gemeinnützig	non-commercial
foundation	Stiftung	→ to found
to donate	spenden	→ donation
to encourage	unterstützen, fördern, ermutigen	= to support
effort	Mühe, Leistung, Versuch	= attempt
improvement	Verbesserung	→ to improve
realisation	Verwirklichung, Realisierung, Erkenntnis	e.g. the realisation of a project; → to realise → real
control	Kontrolle	→ to control
to avoid	(ver)meiden	e.g. We have to avoid environmental disasters.
to cut	senken, verringern, kürzen	= to reduce

= synonym ↔ opposite → word family

Food and food production		
menu	Speisekarte	Waiter, what's on the menu today?
seafood	Fisch und Meeresfrüchte	Seafood is healthy.
tuna, pl. tuna	Thunfisch	a large fish that lives in warm seas and is caught for food
salmon, pl. salmon	Lachs	a tasty kind of fish which looks pink when you cut it open
king prawn	Königskrabbe	seafood, similar to a shrimp but bigger
beef	Rindfleisch	meat that comes from cows
˙cattle	Vieh	cows and bulls
protein	Protein, Eiweiß	Protein can be found in meat, fish, eggs and milk.
pineapple	Ananas	a fruit
banana	Banane	a fruit
exotic	exotisch	e.g. Curry is an exotic dish.
vegetable	Gemüse	e.g. broccoli, cauliflower, carrot
˙rice	Reis	Risotto is made with rice.
˙maize	Mais	a tall plant that produces sweetcorn
calorie	Kalorie	If you work hard you use up more calories.
home food related	im Zusammenhang mit der häuslichen Nahrungszubereitung	connected with food preparation at home
agriculture	Landwirtschaft	= farming
fertiliser	Dünger	It makes plants grow.
˙seed	Saat, Samen	A lot of plants grow from seeds.
˙harvest	Ernte	In the autumn the farmers usually bring in the harvest.
non-food	Nichtlebensmittel, Güter, die nicht zum Verzehr gedacht sind	↔ food

= synonym ↔ opposite → word family

1 Word building: Match the parts of the words from the boxes and form words. One word has been done for you to help you get started.

~~rain~~ • bio • wild • pine • over • country • sea • rain • wilder • bio • con • in

fuel • trol • fishing • side • life • ~~fall~~ • reserve • crease • apple • ness • forest • food

rainfall		

2 Which words from exercise 1 correspond with these definitions?

a) Catching too many fish in a particular area of the sea: ....

b) A large area of land where people have never built or grown anything: ....

c) Land outside cities and towns with forests, fields and grasslands: ....

d) Animals that live on their own in natural conditions, not near people: ....

e) An area where animals and plants are protected: ....

3 Work out the anagrams and write down the words.

a) ANOSSE ....

b) VIROCANSENOT ....

c) SARCTYL ....

d) PITLIOXATONE ....

e) LYNCRICEG ....

f) GALEA ....

g) OGELYCO ....

h) STREED ....

i) AGWESE ....

j) VETRONPIMEM ....

4 Use five words from exercise 3 to complete these sentences.

a) .... is the study of interactions between organisms, such as plants and animals, with the environment.

b) If we don't stop the .... of nature, there will be even more natural catastrophes such as wild storms and floods in the future.

c) Introducing a low emission zone in our city has been an environmental ....

d) The .... of existing ecosystems is one of the major focuses of environmental organizations and green parties.

e) Well-run .... programs cost less than collecting rubbish and then depositing it in landfills or burning it.

5 Fill in the gaps with these verb forms.

aims harms identify run out contribute provide

a) How long will the Earth .... us with oil and coal?

b) What will happen if we .... of these fuels in a few decades?

c) Transporting food over long distances .... the environment.

d) Greenpeace .... to preserve the diversity of the Earth.

e) Most people can .... with this goal, but some criticize the organization's direct actions.

f) There are many simple ways in which you can .... to saving energy and protecting nature.

6 Match the synonyms and write down the pairs.

disaster | nuclear | issue | to emit | to encourage

to cut | negative | catastrophe | agriculture | to reduce

farming | natural | toxic | atomic | worried

to give out | intact | to support | bad | topic

poisonous | organic | concerned | unspoiled

7 Match the sentence parts.

1. Your responsibility
2. If you need assistance,
3. A concern
4. Complex problems
5. When you are able to realise a plan
6. Most foundations
7. Regular donations of money or goods
8. If you make a real effort,
9. Your conscience tells you

a) are often difficult to solve.
b) you try hard to do something difficult.
c) are non-profit organizations.
d) someone has to help you.
e) are a form of social commitment.
f) whether actions are good or bad.
g) is your job or your duty.
h) you achieve the result that you expected.
i) is an issue that worries you.

1. 2. 3. 4. 5. 6. 7. 8. 9.

8 **Combine these phrases with the words in the list. Then translate the expressions you have formed into German.**

carbon global natural solar nuclear fossil

sustainable low-flush non-profit non-food organic

	fuel	*fossiler Brennstoff*
	toilet	
	manufacturing	
	energy	
	farming	
	resources	
	dioxide	
	organization	
	development	
	waste	
	warming	

9 **Find words on page 39 to fill in the gaps. Sometimes you have to use plural forms.**

a) Pineapples and ______________ are ______________ fruit.

b) In this bistro, you can find risotto made with organic ______________ on the ______________ .

c) Fish is high in ______________, but environmentalists warn people against eating too many endangered kinds of fish, such as ______________ or ______________ .

d) You should not consume too much ______________, either, because large areas of rainforest are destroyed in order to raise more and more cattle.

e) The use of chemical ______________ in agriculture has increased steadily during the last few decades.

Unit 7

Man and technology

Technology		
˙technological	technisch, technologisch	→ technology
installation	Installation, Anlage, Einrichtung	→ to install
power plant	Kraftwerk	= power station
power	Energie, Strom	→ to power → powerful
˙electricity	Elektrizität	→ electrician → electric
hydro power	Wasserkraft	Hydro power is used to make electricity in a power station.
hydrogen	Wasserstoff	a gas you produce from water
renewable	erneuerbar	→ new
exhaustible	begrenzt, sich erschöpfend	= limited
steam	Dampf	When water boils you get steam.
steam engine	Dampfmaschine, Dampflokomotive	e.g. The modern steam engine was designed by James Watt.
˙turbine	Turbine	Turbines produce electricity.
blade	Flügel, Blatt, Klinge	e.g. A modern wind turbine usually has two or three blades.
magnet	Magnet	a piece of iron which attracts iron
power line	Starkstromleitung, Überlandleitung	a line that provides places with electricity
hybrid	Hybrid-	e.g. A hybrid car has a petrol engine and an electric motor.
wind farm	Windpark	e.g. You can find many wind farms near the coast.

= synonym ↔ opposite → word family

Online Link
800041-0007

Biotechnology		
childless	kinderlos	not having any children of one's own
human	menschlich	of people or typical of people; e.g. the human body, the human brain
being	(Lebe-)Wesen, Geschöpf	→ to be
embryo	Embryo	→ embryonic
· embryonic-like	wie von einem Embryo	resembling an embryo
to clone	klonen	→ cloning → clone
duplicate	Duplikat, Kopie	= copy; → duplication → to duplicate
biotechnology	Biotechnologie	the use of living organisms e.g. in the production of medicine
scientific	wissenschaftlich	→ science → scientist
DNA	DNS, DNA (Träger der Erbinformation)	*(short form of)* deoxyribonucleic acid
· cell	Zelle	very small structure in the body
· stem cell	Stammzelle	an unspecialized cell that can develop into different cells
· tissue	Gewebe	a large number of cells which have the same function
lab	Labor(atorium)	*(short form of)* laboratory
genetic	genetisch, Gen-	→ gene
to give birth to	zur Welt bringen, gebären	She gave birth to a sweet little girl.
fertility	Fruchtbarkeit	→ fertile
in-vitro fertilisation	In-vitro-Befruchtung (im Reagenzglas)	In-vitro fertilisation (IVF) takes place in a laboratory.
deadly	tödlich	→ death → to die → dead
disease	Krankheit	illness, often caused by infection
· breakthrough	Durchbruch	an important change or development
· applicable	anwendbar, durchführbar	→ application → to apply

= synonym ↔ opposite → word family

Body		
organ	Organ	part of your body, e.g. your heart
bone	Knochen	There are 206 bones in the body.
bone marrow	Knochenmark	the inside part of a bone
liver	Leber	an organ
transplant	Transplantation, Übertragung	→ transplantation → to transplant
gene	Gen, Erbfaktor	→ genetic
skin	Haut	The organ that covers your body.
stomach	Magen	e.g. You shouldn't go swimming on a full stomach.
conscious	bewusst, bei Bewusstsein	= aware, awake; → consciousness
dehydrated	entwässert, dehydriert	the condition of having lost too much water from your body
lung	Lunge	a breathing organ
vomit	Erbrochenes	→ to vomit
Religion and ethics		
God	Gott	You hear about God at church.
religion	Religion, Glaube	→ religious
prayer	Gebet	→ to pray
tolerance	Toleranz	→ to tolerate → tolerant
Muslim (also Moslem)	Muslim(in)	a person who believes in Islam
Jewish	jüdisch	→ Jew
ethics	Moral, ethische Grundsätze	moral prinicples
ethical	ethisch, moralisch	= moral; ↔ unethical
fate	Schicksal	what happens to you
value	Wert	a principle by which you live
blessing	Segen	a prayer asking for God's protection, or: benefit, advantage; → to bless
curse	Fluch	evil, disadvantage; → to curse
truthful	ehrlich	= honest; → truth

= synonym ↔ opposite → word family

Exercises

1 Word building: Form expressions with the parts of the words from the boxes.

steam • power • in-vitro • bone • stem • wind • hydro • power

line • farm • plant • engine • cell • fertilisation • power • marrow

2 Read the clues and complete the grid.

1 The hot gas that is produced when water boils
2 The quality of energy that can easily be produced again as soon as it has been used
3 A form of energy that you can use to produce light or heat, for example
4 The same as limited
5 A machine with a wheel or engine which is turned by number 1, or by water or wind
6 The same as number 3
7 Flat parts that turn around in an engine and push back air or water
8 A gas that is part of water (chemical symbol: H)
9 A piece of iron that attracts other objects made of iron
10 Using two types of energy

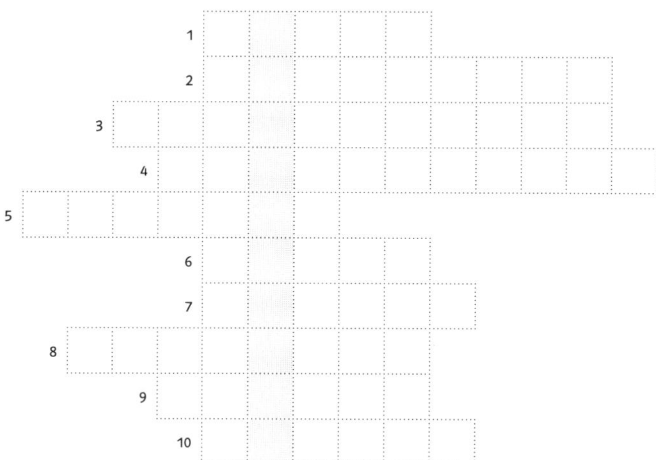

3 **Word families: Write down the corresponding nouns or adjectives. Then use a dictionary to add the German translation of each word.**

Noun	Adjective
electricity – *Elektrizität*	
	technological –
embryo –	
	applicable –
science –	
	truthful –
fertility –	
	ethical –
death –	
	tolerant –
religion –	
	conscious –

4 **Complete the words. You can find all of them on page 45.**

a) Chinese s…… i…… n…… s have found a new way of …… l…… n…… g c…… s.

b) They converted skin c…… s taken from mice into e…… -like c…… s.

c) Until then it had only been possible to d…… p…… t…… animals, but with the new methods specific body …… i…… es can be produced as well now.

d) This has been a b…… thr…… in b…… t…… n…… y.

e) At the moment the new techniques are not a…… l…… le to h…… n c…… s yet, but experts say that it will only be a matter of time until h…… n b…… s will be produced.

f) However, a lot of people believe that it should never be possible to produce babies in a l…… b…… .

5 Complete the sentences with these words.

stomach | skin | bones | vomit | lungs
transplantation | dehydrated | organ (2x) | genes

a) ______ have a soft centre, called marrow, where blood cells are produced.

b) In a ______ an ______ is either moved from one body to another, or from a donor site to a patient's body.

c) Smoking damages your ______.

d) If you eat too much, your ______ may hurt.

e) People with food poisoning often have to ______.

f) Does talent lie all in the ______?

g) Try to drink at least two litres of water every day because being ______ can cause headaches and other pains.

h) The ______ is the outer covering of the body and our largest ______.

6 Match the expressions on the left with the correct German translations. Try to guess if you are not sure.

1. the will of God
2. to say a prayer
3. blows of fate
4. moral values
5. both a blessing and a curse
6. moment of truth

a) Wehen des Schicksals
b) Moment der Erkenntnis
c) moralische Wertvorstellungen
d) Stunde der Wahrheit
e) der Wille Gottes
f) wertvolle Moral
g) ein Gebet sprechen
h) Segen und Fluch
i) Schicksalsschläge

1. 2. 3. 4. 5. 6.

Unit 8

The tourist industry

Tourism		
tourism	Tourismus	→ tourist
catalogue	Katalog	a book with a list of things you can buy
travel	das Reisen	→ traveller → to travel
destination	Ziel, Reiseziel	place to which you are going
faraway	fern, weit entfernt	↔ near, close
booking	Buchung, Reservierung	→ to book
airline	Fluggesellschaft	a company that owns planes and organizes air travel
to depart	abfliegen, abfahren	→ departure
overnight	über Nacht	e.g. an overnight flight
to hire	mieten	= to rent
resort	Ferienort, Badeort	a popular place to go on holiday
attraction	Attraktion, Anziehungspunkt	→ to attract → attractive
sightseeing	Besichtigungstour	looking at tourist attractions
guide	Führer(in)	a person or a book that gives information; → to guide
fascinating	faszinierend	→ fascination → to fascinate
surroundings	Umgebung	the world around us
adventure	Abenteuer	e.g. adventure holidays in Africa; → adventurer → adventurous
infrastructure	Infrastruktur	the system of a country with regard to transport, energy supply, communication etc.
accessible	zugänglich, befahrbar	→ access

= synonym ↔ opposite → word family

Online Link
800041-0008

Nature and environment		
nature	Natur	→ natural
forest	Wald	an area covered with trees, usually larger than a wood
˙jungle	Dschungel	a wild area of land; e.g. the rainforest
barrier reef	der Küste vorgelagertes Riff	e.g. The Great Barrier Reef is near the coast of Australia.
˙coastal	Küsten-	→ coast
˙plain	Ebene, Fläche	a wide, open space
volcano, pl. volcanoes	Vulkan	→ volcanic
thermal	Thermal-, Wärme-	producing or caused by heat
spring	Quelle, Brunnen	water coming from the earth
wild	wild	↔ tame
alive	lebendig	→ life → to live
untouched	unberührt, unversehrt	→ touch → to touch
peaceful	friedlich	→ peace
˙survival	Überleben	→ survivor → to survive
bioreserve	(Bio-)Reservat	an area where nature is protected
to preserve	bewahren, erhalten, schonen	→ preservation → a preserve
bin	Mülleimer, Mülltonne	= garbage can *(AE)*
litter	Abfall	= rubbish *(BE)*; garbage *(AE)*
˙pesticide	Schädlingsbekämpfungsmittel, Pflanzenschutzmittel	chemical specifically used to kill harmful insects
˙carbon	Kohlenstoff	element in coal or petroleum
˙footprint	Fußabdruck	a mark that is left in earth or sand by a foot
˙carbon footprint	CO_2-Bilanz, CO_2-Fußabdruck	a measurement of the amount of carbon dioxide (CO_2) that people produce
˙exhaust	Abgas	emissions from a car or plane

= synonym ↔ opposite → word family

Economy		
sector	Sektor	= part
primary	primär, hauptsächlich, Erst-	= first
secondary	sekundär, Zweit-	→ second
tertiary	tertiär, Dritt-	= third
˙ economic	ökonomisch, wirtschaftlich	→ economy
˙ economical	wirtschaftlich, sparsam	being careful with money, resources, etc.
˙ industrial	industriell	→ industry
˙ corporation	Aktiengesellschaft	→ corporate
˙ budget	Haushalt, Etat	→ to budget → budgetary
investor	Kapitalanleger, Investor	→ investment
˙ transaction	Übertragung, Transaktion, Geschäft	an item of business
to establish	aufbauen, (be)gründen	→ establishment
˙ to finance	finanzieren	→ finance (e.g. public finance)
˙ to thrive	Erfolg haben, gedeihen, blühen	e.g. A thriving business can bring a lot of money into a town.
extraction	Gewinnung, Förderung, Entnahme	taking raw materials out of the ground; → to extract
mining	Bergbau	→ (coal) mine → miner → to mine
˙ to lobby for s.th.	sich für etwas einsetzen	→ lobbyist
˙ businessman	Geschäftsmann	→ business
˙ operative	angelernte(r) Arbeiter(in)	a skilled worker
˙ inflation	Inflation, Geldentwertung	If a country introduces too much money, inflation may rise.
˙ corruption	Korruption, Bestechlichkeit	→ corrupt
˙ bankrupt	bankrott, insolvent	→ bankruptcy
˙ non-working	nicht erwerbstätig	not having a job

= synonym ↔ opposite → word family

Sports		
sporting	sportlich, Sport-	→ sport
jet-skiing	Wassermotorrad fahren	going by jet-ski
paragliding	Gleitschirm fahren	a special way of flying
to hike	wandern	→ hiking → hiker
motorboat	Motorboot	a boat with an engine or a motor
to float	mit dem Floß fahren, treiben, gleiten	to move on a river; → float
· ice hockey	Eishockey	a game played on ice with long sticks and a disc called a puck
· gymnastics	Gymnastik, Turnen	exercises done in a sports hall or gym
· freestyle	Freistil, Kür	A sports competition in which all kinds of movement are allowed.
· aerobics	Aerobic	exercises, often performed in a group and to music, which make the heart, lungs and muscles stronger
· parkour	Parkour, schnelle Fortbewegung ohne Hilfsmittel	a sport in which you try to move as quickly as possible by running, jumping and climbing
· ballroom dancing	Gesellschaftstanz	a formal kind of dancing
· to balance	balancieren	to keep your body in a certain position without falling over
· to swing	schwingen, schaukeln	→ the swing
· to stretch	dehnen, strecken	Before you do any sport you should do some stretching exercises.
· to tackle	angreifen	→ tackle (in football, rugby)
· coordination	Koordination, Abstimmung	e.g. To be good at sport your hand-eye coordination must be good.
· gym	Sporthalle	= sports hall, *(short form of)* gymnasium

= synonym ↔ opposite → word family

Exercises

1 What do you call the people described here?

A person who …

a) almost died but continues to live: ....

b) visits a place for pleasure, usually on holiday: ....

c) goes to other places, either for pleasure or on business: ....

d) goes for long walks in the countryside for pleasure: ....

e) enjoys exciting or dangerous experiences: ....

f) leads you through a place and gives you information: ....

2 Find the words on pages 50 and 51 that correspond with the definitions.

a) A mountain which sometimes emits hot material: ....

b) Not changed or damaged by anything: ....

c) A word used to describe places that you can reach easily: ....

d) Quiet and calm: ....

e) To leave from: ....

f) A container for litter: ....

g) The systems a country needs in order to work effectively: ....

h) An area covered with trees: ....

i) A line of rocks in the water near a coast: ....

j) Not dead: ....

k) An arrangement that you make before you go on holiday: ....

3 **Read the text and work out the anagrams. Write down the correct words below. Then add the German translations.**

My parents and I love to (1) VALRET. When we plan our summer holidays we always spend many hours studying (2) EGOLACUSTA and discussing which (3) NINITEDASOT is the most (4) VATICRETAT. Dad would love to go (5) AWARFYA places such as China or New Zealand, but Mum hates long journeys, especially (6) NIGVROTEH flights. So we usually go to southern Europe. Last summer we went to a beautiful (7) TERORS in Spain. You could do so many things there: relax on the beach, do (8) TOGIRPSN activities, or go for (9) GEGISTSIHEN tours. We visited Jerez and Cadiz, which are (10) SAGNIFITCAN places.

(1) ....

(2) ....

(3) ....

(4) ....

(5) ....

(6) ....

(7) ....

(8) ....

(9) ....

(10) ....

4 **Mark the word in each row that does not go with the others. Explain your choice.**

a) carbon – air – exhaust – pesticide ....

b) airline – resort – opera house – sight ....

c) attractive – sightseeing – fascinating – popular ....

d) wood – reef – jungle – forest ....

e) coastal – volcanic – preserve – thermal ....

5 **Complete the sentences with these words.**

preserve | wild | extraction | bioreserves

survival | carbon footprint | Springs

a) .... are home to a large number of .... animals.

b) Hot .... National Park in Arkansas features 62° thermal waters.

c) If you want to .... nature, avoid producing too much rubbish.

d) You can find different calculators on the Internet to estimate your .... and see how much CO_2 your lifestyle creates each year.

e) Accidents in oil .... can cause severe pollution.

f) A number of leading scientists say that the .... of our planet depends on our ability to tackle the problems of climate change.

6 **Word families: Write down the corresponding nouns or adjectives. Then use a dictionary to add the German translation of each word.**

Noun	**Adjective**
corruption – *Korruption, Bestechlichkeit*	
	economic –
budget –	
	bankrupt –
industry –	
	corporate –

Explain the difference between 'economic' and 'economical'.

....

....

7 Match the sentence parts.

1. The economy includes
2. The primary sector
3. The secondary sector
4. The tertiary sector
5. An investor
6. Mining is
7. If you lobby for something,
8. A thriving business
9. In a transaction
10. Financing something
11. If you establish a firm

a) deals with the production of goods.
b) the extraction of coal or metals from the ground.
c) you try to persuade a politician or the government that something should happen or not.
d) means providing money for it.
e) involves the extraction and production of raw materials.
f) you found it.
g) something is sold or money is exchanged.
h) puts money into something in order to make a profit.
i) several sectors.
j) has to do with services to consumers and businesses.
k) is a successful business.

1. 2. 3. 4. 5. 6. 7. 8. 9. 10. 11.

8 Find 17 sports words in this grid.

→ ← ↓ ↑ ↘ ↙

O	B	N	K	P	A	R	A	G	L	I	D	I	N	G	G	C	M	Y	Z
T	A	O	L	F	C	G	P	R	U	L	N	X	P	A	R	K	O	U	R
J	E	H	Y	L	I	N	Y	W	H	C	T	E	R	T	S	Y	T	Z	E
E	R	T	I	X	Y	I	C	O	O	R	D	I	N	A	T	I	O	N	L
T	O	Q	E	K	P	W	R	A	W	A	T	M	R	N	J	B	R	U	Y
S	B	I	W	L	I	S	U	T	A	C	K	L	E	P	A	Z	B	L	T
K	I	C	Y	N	Y	N	X	P	C	Y	L	N	B	L	Z	R	O	W	S
I	C	T	V	R	X	U	G	N	J	B	R	C	A	W	I	W	A	M	E
I	S	U	Y	E	K	C	O	H	E	C	I	N	G	X	Y	N	T	N	E
N	S	C	I	T	S	A	N	M	Y	G	C	U	C	Y	W	Q	M	O	R
G	B	O	C	V	R	S	T	Z	R	E	M	Z	L	O	M	U	Y	V	F
M	Y	N	G	N	I	C	N	A	D	M	O	O	R	L	L	A	B	Z	E

Unit 9

Globalisation and multiculturalism

Global trade		
globalisation	Globalisierung	→ global → to globalise
chance	Chance	e.g. Does globalisation offer chances to poorer countries?
risk	Risiko	→ to risk
standard	Standard, Norm, Maßstab	e.g. ethical standards, fair trade standards
industrialized	industrialisiert	industrialized countries ↔ developing countries
· developing world	Entwicklungsländer	Most people in the developing world are poor.
· dependent (on)	abhängig	→ dependence → to depend ↔ independent
manufacturer	Hersteller	→ manufacturing → to manufacture
merchant	Händler, Kaufmann, Handelsmann	a person who trades products in large amounts
· trader	Händler(in)	→ trade → to trade
to make money	Geld verdienen	to earn a lot of money, to make a profit
logistics	Logistik, Versorgung	having to do with the transportation of goods; → logistic, logistical
guideline	Richtlinie	official advice or rule
to eliminate	beseitigen, entfernen, eliminieren	= to cancel; → elimination
option	Möglichkeit, Alternative	= possibility; → optional
· foreigner	Ausländer(in)	→ foreign

= synonym ↔ opposite → word family

Online Link
800041-0009

Different cultures		
ethnic	ethnisch	An ethnic group shares the same culture, religion, language etc.
authentic	authentisch	= real → authenticity
original	original, ursprünglich, unbearbeitet	→ origin
˙ native	eingeboren, einheimisch	→ native
racial	Rassen-	→ race
diverse	unterschiedlich, vielfältig, verschieden	= different → diversity
mixture	Mischung	→ to mix
˙ multicultural	multikulturell	→ multiculturalism
˙ custom	Gewohnheit, Sitte, Brauch	It is a custom in Scotland that men wear special skirts.
Asian	asiatisch	→ Asia
˙ European	europäisch	→ Europe
˙ North/South American	nord-/südamerikanisch	→ North/South America
˙ African	afrikanisch	→ Africa
˙ Australian	australisch	→ Australia

Exercises

1 **Word families: Fill in the corresponding words.**

Noun	Verb
trader	
	to depend
risk	
	to mix
manufacturing	
	to eliminate
globalisation	

Noun	Adjective
origin	
	logistical
authenticity	
	diverse
race	
	foreign
option	

= synonym ↔ opposite → word family

2 What do these words mean? Tick the right answer.

standard:
a) An opinion you want to defend ☐
b) A rule, often a moral rule, according to which people should act ☐
c) A person's position in a group or in an organization ☐

custom:
a) The amount of money you need to buy, do or make something ☐
b) A sweet yellow sauce that you eat with desserts ☐
c) A certain way of doing things in a society or a community ☐

native:
a) A person who was born in a particular place ☐
b) A country that is considered as a group of people with the same language and traditions ☐
c) A person who is very good at something without having to learn it ☐

manufacturing:
a) The activity of selling products by advertising them ☐
b) Trading products ☐
c) The business of producing large quantities of products, often from raw materials ☐

diversity:
a) A difference in opinion ☐
b) The condition of being different, for example among a range of people ☐
c) The condition of groups of people who are opposed to each other ☐

dependence:
a) The condition of needing something or someone in order to be able to live ☐
b) The condition of being unhappy and without hope ☐
c) The process of growing and changing ☐

3 Complete the sentences.

a) A merchant is a person who ....

b) A foreigner is a person who ....

c) A trader is a person who ....

d) A manufacturer is a person who ....

4 **Write down the names of the continents and the corresponding adjectives.**

Continent	Adjective

5 **Complete the words.**

a) A lot of people think that g....b.l........n has offered the d........p........ world better ....an..... .

b) For example, China is nowadays among the top m........f....t........g countries in the world, and India is m.....ing m...n..... in the services sector.

c) New forms of l..g.........s have been developed in order to manage international trade.

d) Economic cooperation between countries all over the world has also brought about more cultural d.........ty.

e) Thus you can find a m........c........al m.....t........ of people in all the large European and American cities.

f) However, critics say that the g........l economy puts poorer countries at r........ of increasing income inequality and makes them d........d....t on i..d........r........ed countries.

g) Quite a lot of people in poor countries have to work under difficult conditions and they feel exploited by fo........n....s.

h) The Organisation for Economic Co-operation and Development (OECD) points out that human rights, including labour rights, are more important than tr........ rules, and it has therefore issued g........l....es for multinational companies.

Unit 10

International politics

State and government		
democracy	Demokratie	→ democratic
constitution	Verfassung	→ constitutional
unconstitutional	verfassungswidrig	↔ constitutional
president	Präsident	→ presidential
federal	Bundes-	→ federation
parliament	Parlament	→ parliamentary
to make up (s.th.)	etwas bilden, zusammenstellen	e.g. The party makes up over fifty percent of the parliament.
separation of powers	Gewaltenteilung	one of the main principles of democratic states
checks and balances	gegenseitige Kontrolle, Gewaltenteilung	an important part of the US system of government
legislative	legislativ, gesetzgebend	→ legislation
executive	exekutiv, ausführend	The executive branch in politics usually is the government.
judiciary	Judikative, Justizgewalt, Gerichtswesen	→ judicial
Supreme Court	Oberstes Bundesgericht	the highest court in the USA
concentration	Ansammlung, Verdichtung, Konzentration	→ to concentrate
Congress	Kongress (Parlament in den USA)	→ congressional
bill	Gesetzesvorlage	a suggestion for a new law
appointment	Berufung	choosing a person for a position; → to appoint
bureaucracy	Bürokratie	→ bureaucratic

= synonym ↔ opposite → word family

Online Link
800041-0010

The political process		
voter	Wähler(in)	→ to vote
to register	(sich) registrieren, einschreiben, anmelden	e.g. to register to vote; → a register
delegate	Delegierte(r), Abgeordnete(r), Bevollmächtigte(r)	→ to delegate
to represent	repräsentieren, vertreten	= to stand for, to act in place of
majority	Mehrheit	↔ minority
to limit	begrenzen	→ limit; e.g. to limit power
indirect	indirekt, mittelbar	↔ direct; e.g. indirect elections
to function	funktionieren	= to work; → function
to pass	(ein Gesetz) verabschieden	to agree on a law
veto	Veto, Einspruchsrecht, Einspruch	→ to veto ↔ approval
to reverse	umkehren	to change back; → reversal
to nominate	ernennen, nominieren, aufstellen	→ nomination
to approve	anerkennen, bestätigen, zustimmen	→ approval
to permit	erlauben, zulassen, genehmigen	= to allow → permission
to declare	erklären	e.g. to declare war; → declaration
to by-pass	umgehen, überbrücken	To by-pass a law is to break it.
referendum	Referendum, Abstimmung, Volksbefragung	a direct vote in which citizens say "yes" or "no" to a special issue
hostile	feindlich	→ hostility ↔ friendly
opponent	Gegner(in)	↔ supporter → opposition → to oppose → opposite
commissioner	Beauftragte(r), Bevollmächtigte(r)	a person who acts officially for his/her government
to orientate	orientieren, ausrichten	→ orientation
to implement	ausführen, verwirklichen, realisieren	= to carry out, to fulfil; → implementation

= synonym ↔ opposite → word family

International politics		
peacekeeping	Friedenserhaltung, Friedensbewahrung	making sure that a war does not break out
operation	Operation, Handlung	= act, action, activity
commander-in-chief	Oberbefehlshaber	the top leader of the military
leader	Führer(in)	→ to lead
armed forces	Militär, Streitkräfte	airforce, army and navy
treaty	Vertrag	an official agreement between countries or nations
international	international	concerning two or more countries
intergovernmental	zwischenstaatlich, international	= international
enlargement	Vergrößerung, Erweiterung, Erhöhung	e.g. the enlargement of the EU; → to enlarge
continent	Kontinent, Erdteil	e.g. Europe is a continent.
stable	stabil	↔ unstable; → stability
countryman	Landsmann	s.o. who comes from your country
potential	potenziell, eventuell	= possible → potential
accession	Beitritt, Einwilligung, Zuwachs	the point at which a country becomes a member of an organization
criterion, *pl.* criteria	Kriterium, Kriterien	= standard
ally	Alliierte(r), Verbündete(r)	= partner, friend
to disappear	verschwinden	→ disappearance
to afford	sich leisten	to be able to buy or do s.th.
European Monetary Union	Europäische Wirtschafts- und Währungsunion	*(short form)* = EMU
institution	Institution, Einrichtung	e.g. The European Commission is an institution of the EU.
council	Gremium, Rat	= committee
European Court of Justice	Europäischer Gerichtshof	the highest court in the EU

= synonym ↔ opposite → word family

Humanitarian aid		
United Nations	Vereinte Nationen	*(short form)* = UN
humanitarian	humanitär, menschenfreundlich	→ humanity → human
aid	Hilfe	= help; → to aid
to prevent s.th. from happening/s.o. from doing s.th.	verhindern	e.g. to prevent diseases from breaking out; → prevention
non-governmental	nichtregierungs-, nichtstaatlich	non-governmental organization = NGO
ration	Zuteilung, Ration	a limited amount; → to ration
to escape (from)	flüchten (vor)	→ escape
to flee, fled, fled	fliehen	= to escape, to run away
condition	Zustand, Situation	e.g. poor living conditions
illiterate	des Lesens und Schreibens unkundig	→ literate
desperate	verzweifelt, aussichtslos	→ despair → to despair
to persecute	verfolgen	→ persecution → persecutor
slum	Slum, Elendsviertel	poor area of a town
belongings	Habseligkeiten, Eigentum	→ to belong
refuge	Asyl, Zufluchtsstätte	a place where you can go if you are in danger; → refugee
migration	Migration, Abwanderung, Umzug	→ migrant → to migrate ↔ immigration
tragedy	Tragödie	→ tragic
slave	Sklave/Sklavin	→ slavery
short-term	kurzfristig, befristet, kurzzeitig	↔ long-term; e.g. short-term projects
committee	Komitee, Ausschuss, Gremium	e.g. The committee decided to help poor children in Africa.
zone	Zone, Gebiet, Bereich	= area; e.g. war zone
to arrange	organisieren, ausmachen	→ arrangement
to carry out	ausführen	= to do s.th., to complete s.th.

= synonym ↔ opposite → word family

Exercises

1 Match the synonyms and write down the pairs.

to represent | to carry out | to flee | zone | to implement | aid

ally | to function | to complete | operation | standard | committee

to fulfil | to escape | help | partner | to stand for | area

to permit | council | to work | action | to allow | criterion

2 Write down the opposites.

hostile ↔ ....

majority ↔ ....

direct ↔ ....

veto ↔ ....

supporter ↔ ....

stable ↔ ....

long-term ↔ ....

constitutional ↔ ....

3 Complete the sentences.

a) A commissioner is a person who ....

b) A commander-in-chief is ....

c) A countryman is ....

4 **Find six noun-verb pairs in the lists on pages 63 to 65 that have the same forms. Then use a dictionary to add the German translation of each word.**

Noun	Verb

5 **Word families: Fill in the corresponding nouns or adjectives. Then use a dictionary to add the German translation of each word.**

Noun	**Adjective**
legislation – *Legislative, Gesetzgebung*	
	judicial –
federation –	
	bureaucratic –
tragedy –	

6 **Complete the sentences with verbs from this unit.**

a) If a parliament agrees on a bill, it ______ the bill.

b) To by-pass a law means to ______ it.

c) If you change something back, you ______ it.

d) When people say yes to a proposal, they ______ it.

e) To ______ a person means to choose the person to do a particular job.

f) If you are able to buy something, you can ______ it.

g) If you ______ an event, you plan and organize it.

7 What do these words mean? Tick the right answer.

delegate:
a) A person who stands in for a leader or manager while he or she is away ☐
b) A person who is voted for and then represents the voters' interests ☐
c) A leader of a political party ☐

to persecute:
a) To accuse a person of committing a crime in a court ☐
b) To continue doing something, even if you have extreme problems ☐
c) To treat people in a cruel or unfair way, especially because of their religion, race or political opinions ☐

illiterate:
a) Not having a formal education ☐
b) Not being able to read and write ☐
c) Knowing nothing about literature ☐

despair:
a) The feeling you have when you have lost all hope ☐
b) The inability to help other people ☐
c) A very difficult situation ☐

hostility:
a) Unfriendly or aggressive behaviour ☐
b) Very friendly behaviour towards guests ☐
c) A feeling of great shock or fear ☐

8 Match the sentence parts.

1. The Supreme Court
2. The separation of powers is
3. Checks and balances
4. When states or communities work together at the international level,
5. EMU
6. The European Court of Justice

a) is a division into three branches: executive, legislative and judicial.
b) is the short form of European Monetary Union.
c) we call this intergovernmental cooperation.
d) is a term used in the American constitution for the separation of powers.
e) is the highest court in the EU.
f) is the highest court in the United States.

1. 2. 3. 4. 5. 6.

9 **Complete the sentences with these words.**

refuge | slums | migrated | conditions | humanitarian
prevent | rations | persecution | declarations

a) The United Nations was established after World War II in order to ………… further international aggressions and ………… of war.

b) The UN undertook its first ………… aid operations in Europe.

c) The living ………… in urban ………… are characterized by poor hygiene and violence.

d) Throughout history, people have ………… for a variety of reasons: poverty, religious …………, or lack of political freedom.

e) Turkey has become a ………… for people fleeing from Iran.

f) Providing large numbers of refugees with food ………… is a logistical challenge.

10 **Make expressions that correspond with the German phrases.**

non-governmental • safety • refugee • desperate • personal • short-term • peacekeeping • armed	situation • measures • forces • zone • mission • belongings • organization • camp

………… – *Friedensmission*

………… – *verzweifelte Lage*

………… – *Streitkräfte*

………… – *Flüchtlingslager*

………… – *Nichtregierungsorganisation*

………… – *persönliche Habe*

………… – *Sicherheitszone*

………… – *kurzfristige Maßnahmen*

11 Translate the clues and write the English words in the crossword.

Across:
- 4 ausrichten
- 5 verschwinden
- 10 Ansammlung
- 12 Vertrag
- 13 ausführend
- 14 Ausschuss

Down:
- 1 Verfassung
- 2 Demokratie
- 3 Volksbefragung
- 6 Beitritt
- 7 Berufung
- 8 Wähler
- 9 Gesetzesvorlage
- 11 Erweiterung

Units 11–14

Cross-cultural communication

Meeting and talking to people		
conversation	Gespräch, Unterhaltung, Konversation	When people talk to each other, they have a conversation.
to shake	schütteln	e.g. to shake hands
pleased	erfreut	= happy = glad
informal	informell	↔ formal
response	Reaktion, Antwort	= reaction, answer; → to respond
to be in touch	in Verbindung stehen, in Kontakt bleiben	e.g. We'll be in touch.
emotional	emotional, gefühlvoll	→ emotion
intense	angestrengt, intensiv	→ intensity
to confirm	bestätigen, bestärken	→ confirmation
to inquire	sich erkundigen, fragen	→ inquiry
to give s.o.'s regards to s.o.	Grüße ausrichten	Please give Daniel my regards.
to give s.o. a buzz	jemanden anrufen	*(colloquial)* = to call s.o.
caller	Anrufer(in)	→ to call
busy	besetzt, belegt	e.g. The line is busy right now.
to catch s.th.	etwas akustisch verstehen	to hear and understand s.th.
to take a seat	Platz nehmen	= to sit down
inconvenience	Unannehmlichkeit, Belästigung	e.g. Sorry for the inconvenience; → inconvenient
pleasant	angenehm	e.g. Have a pleasant stay.
Take care.	Pass auf dich auf.	Friends say goodbye like this.
What a pity!	Wie schade!	= Too bad!
to cut a long story short	langer Rede kurzer Sinn	to say it briefly

= synonym ↔ opposite → word family

Online Link
800041-0011

Writing letters and e-mails		
draft	Entwurf, Skizze	→ draftsman → to draft
reference	Referenz, Bezug	a letter that is written by s.o. who knows you to say you are suitable for a job; or: s.th. you refer to for information
˙to refer (to)	sich beziehen auf	→ reference
salutation	Begrüßung, Anrede	You always start a letter with a salutation.
request	Nachfrage, Anfrage	→ to request
apology	Entschuldigung	→ to apologize
˙polite	höflich	↔ impolite → politeness
to thank	danken, (sich) bedanken	e.g. I would like to thank you for inviting me.
to appreciate	schätzen	→ appreciation
to be delighted	glücklich sein, sehr zufrieden sein	to be very happy; e.g. We will be delighted to have you here at the Thistle Hotel.
sincerely	Mit freundlichen Grüßen	Yours sincerely = Yours faithfully
complimentary close	Grußformel	Yours ...; Yours sincerely ...; Sincerely ...; Kind regards ... are examples of complimentary closes.
attachment	Anhang, Anbringung	→ to attach
dot	Punkt	= full stop; e.g. A sentence ends with a dot.
˙colloquial	umgangssprachlich	informal, everyday language; e.g. You can use colloquial expressions in e-mails to friends.
˙bracket	Klammer	These are brackets: ( ).
˙letter	Buchstabe	e.g. In English letters and e-mails the first word after the salutation starts with a capital letter.

= synonym ↔ opposite → word family

Working in a hotel		
single	einzeln, einfach	e.g. a single room
double	Doppel-, doppelt	e.g. a double room
vacancy	Leere, Lücke	→ vacant
to accommodate	unterbringen	→ accommodation
to check in	einchecken, anmelden	↔ to check out
to charge	in Rechnung stellen, berechnen	e.g. How much do you charge for breakfast?
rate	Preis, Rate	= price
check *(AE)*	Rechnung (im Restau-rant), Scheck	e.g. Can we have the check, please?
bill	Rechnung, Banknote	→ to bill
reduction	Reduzierung	→ to reduce
availability	Verfügbarkeit	→ to avail → available
stay	Aufenthalt	→ to stay
reservation	Reservierung	e.g. a reservation form
security	Sicherheit	→ to secure
expiry	Fälligwerden, Ablauf, Verfall	→ to expire
to require	benötigen	= need to have; → requirement
on duty	im Dienst	e.g. the receptionist on duty
to cover for s.o.	jdn. vertreten	to do s.o. else's job
to be on business	auf Geschäftsreise sein	to travel for business reasons
floor	Stock, Etage	e.g. This hotel has six floors.
foyer	Vorhalle, Foyer	= entrance
executive suite	Führungsloge, Vor-standsetage	The executive suite is usually on the top floor of the building.
general office	Zentrale	e.g. The general office of the hotel is behind the reception.
restroom *(AE)*	Toilette	= toilet *(BE)*
elevator *(AE)*	Aufzug	= lift *(BE)*
full board	Vollpension, Voll-verpflegung	↔ half board

= synonym ↔ opposite → word family

Different cultures		
culture	Kultur	→ cultural
national	national	→ nation → nationality
overseas	Übersee-, in Übersee	If you go to the USA, you go overseas.
unique	einzigartig	→ uniqueness
identifiable	identifizierbar, erkennbar, feststellbar, belegbar	→ identification → to identify
to celebrate	feiern	→ celebration
queue	Warteschlange	→ to queue
Brit *(informal)*	Brite	a person who comes from Britain
Aussie *(informal)*	Australier(in)	= Australian
dress code	Kleiderordnung	what you have to wear
stranger	Fremde(r)	a person you don't know
cosmopolitan atmosphere	weltoffene Atmosphäre	→ a cosmopolitan

Exercises

1 Word families: Fill in the corresponding nouns or verbs.

Noun	Verb
draft	
	to secure
availability	
	to attach
reference	
	to appreciate
reduction	
	to accommodate
identification	
	to respond

Noun	Verb
	to celebrate
requirement	
	to inquire
apology	
	to bill
queue	
	to stay
caller	
	to expire
request	

= synonym ↔ opposite → word family

2 **Choose verbs from exercise 1 to complete these sentences.**

If you …

a) … notice the positive characteristics of something, you ______ it.

b) … send a file with an e-mail, you ______ it.

c) … ______ a text, you write down the first rough version of it.

d) … very politely ask someone to do something, you ______ this.

e) … say that you are sorry for something you have said or done, you ______.

f) … recognize a person and can say who he or she is, you ______ the person.

g) … lower the price of a product, you ______ it.

h) … give someone a buzz, you ______ the person.

3 **Word families: Fill in the corresponding nouns or adjectives.**

Noun	Adjective
emotion	
	polite
inconvenience	
	intense

Noun	Adjective
culture	
	unique
nation	
	vacant

4 **Choose words from exercise 3 to complete these sentences.**

a) A ______ is a free room in a hotel.

b) A thing that is ______ is the only thing of a kind.

c) Something that does not suit you or causes you trouble is an ______.

d) An ______ person is someone who has strong feelings.

e) Something that is very strong or very great is ______.

5 You are doing a work placement. Write down what you say in the following situations.

a) Sie treffen eine Person zum ersten Mal und sagen, dass Sie sich freuen, sie kennen zu lernen.

b) Sie bitten jemanden, Platz zu nehmen.

c) Sie drücken Ihr Bedauern aus, dass etwas nicht geklappt hat.

d) Sie fassen Ihre bisherigen Ausführungen zusammen und leiten dies mit „langer Rede kurzer Sinn“ ein.

e) Sie entschuldigen sich bei Ihrem Gesprächspartner für eine Unannehmlichkeit.

f) Sie richten Mr Wilkinson, dem Chef Ihrer Gesprächspartnerin, Grüße aus.

g) Sie sagen jemandem zum Abschluss eines Gesprächs, dass Sie in Kontakt bleiben.

h) Sie haben bei einem Telefongespräch etwas akustisch nicht verstanden.

i) Sie sagen einem Anrufer, der verbunden werden möchte, dass alle Telefonleitungen besetzt sind.

j) Sie wünschen jemandem einen angenehmen Aufenthalt in Ihrer Stadt.

k) Sie verabschieden sich von einer Kollegin, mit der Sie auch privat zu tun haben.

6 **Use these words to complete the telephone dialogue.**

available | security | stay | charge | single | confirmation

floor (2x) | rate | expiry (2x) | appreciate | reservation

Receptionist: Good morning, Park Hotel, may I help you?

Mrs Parker: Yes, I'd like to make a .... I'd like to .... from 22nd to 24th April.

Receptionist: What kind of room would you like, madam?

Mrs Parker: A ...., please.

Receptionist: Just let me check what we have .... Yes, I could offer you a room on the second .... or one on the fifth.

Mrs Parker: I would .... it if I could have a quiet room.

Receptionist: Well, then the one on the fifth .... should be perfect for you.

Mrs Parker: Good, I'll take it. How much do you .... per night?

Receptionist: Would you like breakfast?

Mrs Parker: Yes, please.

Receptionist: Then the .... is £125 per night, madam.

Mrs Parker: That's fine.

Receptionist: Who's the booking for, please, madam?

Mrs Parker: It's Melanie Parker.

Receptionist: Thank you, Mrs Parker, and as .... we need your credit card number and the .... date, please.

Mrs Parker: Sure. It's a Mastercard and the number is 4286591327859782. The .... date is July 2014.

Receptionist: Thank you very much, Mrs Parker. Now let me give you your .... number. It's 26498715.

Mrs Parker: Good, thank you.

Receptionist: We look forward to having you here. Goodbye, Mrs Parker.

7 Match the sentence parts.

1. Covering for a person
2. Being on duty
3. When you check in at a hotel
4. If you have full board
5. Workers in general offices
6. If a hotel is able to accomodate 350 people,
7. The foyer

a) you go to the reception desk and say that you have arrived.
b) is the entrance of a hotel.
c) all your meals are provided at the hotel.
d) is working at a particular time.
e) it provides rooms and services for this number of guests.
f) is doing the person's job while he or she is away.
g) have to be able to complete a wide range of tasks.

1. 2. 3. 4. 5. 6. 7.

8 Read the clues and complete the grid.

1 A letter always starts with a …
2 You write the … line between the date and number 1
3 You end a letter with a …
4 If you are grateful to a person, you … them.
5 In a formal letter you use this word to express that you are very happy about something.
6 You often put additional information in …, for example dates and time spans.
7 An example of number 3

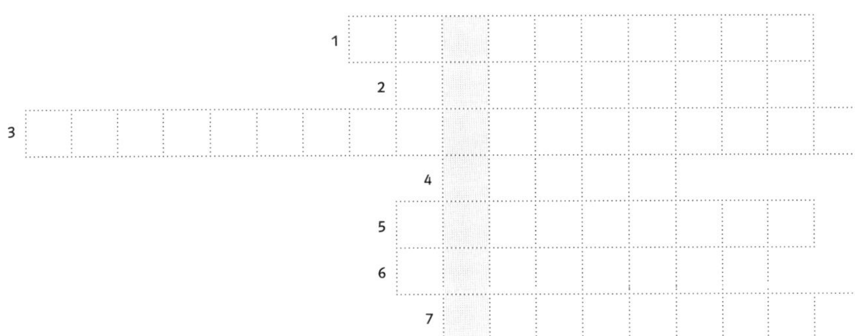

The solution can have two meanings. How can you translate the word?

9 **Use these words to complete the sentences.**

informal | check | colloquial | restrooms | shake | overseas | elevator | intense | dress code | conversations | strangers | cosmopolitan | identifiable

a) New York has a ______ atmosphere because you can meet people from many different parts of the world who either live there or are visitors from ______.

b) In American English the word ' ______ ' is used for 'lift'.

c) If Americans ask you how to find the ______, they are looking for the toilets.

d) When they want to pay in a restaurant they ask for the ______.

e) You can't wear jeans and T-shirts if you are doing a work placement in Britain or the United States, so find out about the ______ before you start.

f) Keep in mind that British people don't ______ hands as often as Germans.

g) If you don't conform to the different habits when staying in another country, you are easily ______ as a foreigner.

h) You shouldn't use ______ expressions in business ______, but you can of course use a few in ______ situations.

i) Never become too emotional or ______ when making small talk to ______.

Key to the exercises

Unit 1: Young people in Europe

1 1 science 2 project 3 fail 4 curriculum 5 attend 6 Geography 7 essay
solution: college

2 impression – to impress residence – to reside coordination – to coordinate
failure – to fail trainee – to train leaver – to leave behaviour – to behave
presentation – to present campaign / campaigning – to campaign
achievement – to achieve

3 a) lifestyle b) subculture c) country of origin d) religion

4 1G 2D 3I 4A 5H 6B 7E 8C 9F

5 (Brendan) National Diploma – social care – placement – nine-to-five job
(Germaine) Information Technology – theoretical
(Damian) apprenticeship – orders – coordination
(Rachel) Geography – part-time job

Unit 2: Getting a job

1 action – to act – active challenge – to challenge – challenging
reward – to reward – rewarding independence – to depend – independent
freezer – to freeze – frozen expansion – to expand – expansive
qualification – to qualify (for) – qualified requirement – to require – requisite

2 challenge: b) manufacturing: c) fluency: a) self-confidence: b)
branch: a) requirement: b) research: c) independence: b)

3 (1) retailer – Einzelhändler (2) expanded – (hat) expandiert (3) chain – Kette
(4) superstore – Megamarkt (5) branches – Niederlassungen
(6) management team – Geschäftsführungsteam (7) turnover – Umsatz
(8) headquarters – Geschäftssitz

4 a) résumé/CV b) a tolerant person c) factory d) tinned

5 1 reliability 2 resilient 3 vacancy 4 permanent 5 curriculum vitae 6 enclosed
7 advert 8 rewarding 9 application 10 long-term 11 requisite 12 open-minded
13 candidate 14 qualified 15 active

O	R	E	W	A	R	D	I	N	G	N	U	H	K	Y	M	U	E	V
T	B	E	A	T	I	V	M	U	L	U	C	I	R	R	U	C	K	A
R	P	Y	C	T	J	S	M	R	E	T	G	N	O	L	I	W	S	C
U	T	N	E	N	A	M	R	E	P	Q	F	V	I	T	C	A	X	A
W	S	E	K	E	F	D	R	M	J	E	N	C	L	O	S	E	D	N
C	A	N	D	I	D	A	T	E	V	W	K	U	E	M	J	H	O	C
H	M	R	K	L	Y	G	H	R	E	L	I	A	B	I	L	I	T	Y
A	P	P	L	I	C	A	T	I	O	N	B	C	L	W	E	Q	U	F
M	G	Y	R	S	E	U	D	E	D	N	I	M	N	E	P	O	W	S
E	A	D	V	E	R	T	E	C	Y	Q	U	A	L	I	F	I	E	D
F	P	S	Y	R	L	E	T	I	S	I	U	Q	E	R	E	F	L	D

6 a) Convenience food b) frozen; tinned c) home-made; sweets
d) groceries; cooking e) recipe

Unit 3: The youth market

1 to prohibit – prohibition to distribute – distribution to promote – promotion
to regulate – regulation to delete – deletion to operate – operation

All the nouns end in -ion. When adding the ending to a verb you have to leave out the final -e.

2 purchase – to purchase bid – to bid range – to range target – to target
label – to label alert – to alert scam – to scam ban – to ban

3 a) target b) ban c) scam d) alert e) label f) bid g) range h) purchase

4 a) trendy (an adjective, not a noun)
b) user (a person, not a mobile phone feature)
c) scam (a crime, not a legal measure)
d) auction (a form of selling, not a form of advertising)
e) flyer (a thing, not a person)

5 1 discount 2 must-have 3 consumer 4 payment 5 inexpensive 6 silver
7 fashionable 8 packaging

6 a) create; brand; promotion b) logo; merchandising c) sponsoring; marketing
d) no-name products; branded; advertised e) Billboards; advertisements; slogans

7 a) features b) prepaid; credit c) text messages d) ringtones; wallpapers e) battery f) premium rate number g) Short codes

8 1.d) 2.f) 3.e) 4.a) 5.c) 6.b)

Unit 4: Media in our lives

1 **Across:** 3 data 5 update 6 wireless 8 keypad 10 button 11 file 12 programming language 13 search engine
Down: 1 games console 2 top-level domain 4 instant messaging 7 icon 9 provider

2 search – to search click – to click killing – to kill witness – to witness comment – to comment conclusion – to conclude summary – to summarize download – to download proposal – to propose report – to report suggestion – to suggest Google – to google

3 a) comment; pros and cons b) context c) summary d) analysis; point out e) suggest f) proposal

4 Suggested answers: a) A judge is a person who decides in court.
b) A murderer is a person who has killed someone.
c) A reporter is a person who informs you about events on the radio or on TV.

5 (1) piracy – *Piraterie* (2) downloaded – *heruntergeladen* (3) stealing – *Stehlen* (4) theft – *Diebstahl* (5) illegal – *illegal* (6) thieves – *Diebe* (7) courts – *Gerichte* (8) files – *Dateien* (9) prison – *Gefängnis*

Unit 5: Social change

1 relationship opportunity interaction feminism function environment racism creativity salary homelessness contraception commitment

2 violence – *Gewalt;* violent – *gewalttätig, brutal*
volunteer – *ehrenamtliche(r) Mitarbeiter(in);* voluntary – *freiwillig, ehrenamtlich*
society – *Gesellschaft;* social – *gesellschaftlich, sozial*
demand – *Forderung;* demanding – *anspruchsvoll*
marriage – *Heirat, Hochzeit;* married – *verheiratet*
beauty – *Schönheit;* beautiful – *schön*
handicap – *Behinderung, Benachteiligung;* handicapped – *behindert, benachteiligt*
convention – *Brauch, Sitte, Konvention;* conventional – *konventionell, normal*
interaction – *Interaktion;* to interact – *interagieren, zusammenwirken*
creativity – *Kreativität;* creative – *kreativ, schöpferisch*
racism – *Rassismus;* racist – *rassistisch*
function – *Funktion, Aufgabe;* functional – *funktional, zweckmäßig*

3 to be pregnant, to be married, to be engaged
to get pregnant, to get married, to get engaged, to get a small wage, to get benefits, to get a high salary
to have a conference, to have a relationship, to have a small wage, to have a handicap, to have a high salary, to have an affair
to become pregnant, to become engaged

to become = *werden; bekommen* = to get

4 a) professions b) commitment; unpaid c) mechanical d) labour e) opportunities f) Shift g) routine; organized h) motivation; commitment; tasks i) interact; organizational j) conference

5 a) contraception; pregnancies b) condoms c) feminist d) female beauty e) engaged; marry f) wedding; honeymoon g) relationship h) partnership i) single parents

6 1E 2G 3A 4I 5H 6D 7F 8C 9B

7 **Across:** 4 childcare 7 homelessness 8 society 9 racism 10 bullying
Down: 1 environment 2 binge drinking 3 benefit 5 anti-social 6 welfare

8 a) primary school; secondary school b) comprehensive schools c) coaching d) special needs

Unit 6: Ecology

1 rainfall biofuel wildlife pineapple overfishing countryside seafood rainforest wilderness bioreserve control increase

2 a) overfishing b) wilderness c) countryside d) wildlife e) bioreserve

3 a) season b) conservation c) crystal d) exploitation e) recycling f) algae g) ecology h) desert i) sewage j) improvement

4 a) Ecology b) exploitation c) improvement d) conservation e) recycling

5 a) provide b) run out c) harms d) aims e) identify f) contribute

6 disaster – catastrophe nuclear – atomic issue – topic to emit – to give out
to encourage – to support to cut – to reduce agriculture – farming
negative – bad natural – organic toxic – poisonous worried – concerned
intact – unspoiled

7 1.g) 2.d) 3.i) 4.a) 5.h) 6.c) 7.e) 8.b) 9.f)

8 fossil fuel – *fossiler Brennstoff* low-flush toilet – *Toilette mit geringem Wasserverbrauch*
non-food manufacturing– *Herstellung von Gütern, die nicht zum Verzehr gedacht sind*
solar energy – *Sonnenenergie/Solarenergie*

organic farming – *biologische Landwirtschaft/ökologischer Landbau*
natural resources – *natürliche Ressourcen/Bodenschätze/Rohstoffe*
carbon dioxide – *Kohlendioxyd/*CO_2 non-profit organization – *gemeinnützige Organisation*
sustainable development – *nachhaltige Entwicklung*
nuclear waste– *Atommüll/Nuklearabfall*
global warming – *globale Erwärmung/Erderwärmung*

9 a) bananas; exotic b) rice; menu c) protein; tuna; salmon d) beef e) fertilisers

Unit 7: Man and technology

1 steam engine power line in-vitro fertilisation bone marrow stem cell wind farm hydo power power plant

2 1 steam 2 renewable 3 electricity 4 exhaustible 5 turbine 6 power 7 blades 8 hydrogen 9 magnet 10 hybrid Solution: technology

3 electricity – *Elektrizität;* electric – *elektrisch* technology – *Technik, Technologie;* technological – *technisch, technologisch* embryo – *Embryo;* embryonic – *embryonal* application – *Anwendung, Durchführung;* applicable – *anwendbar, durchführbar* science – *Wissenschaft;* scientific – *wissenschaftlich* truth – *Wahrheit;* truthful – *ehrlich* fertility – *Fruchtbarkeit;* fertile – *fruchtbar* ethics – *Moral, ethische Grundsätze;* ethical – *ethisch, moralisch* death – *Tod;* dead – *tot;* deadly – *tödlich* tolerance – *Toleranz;* tolerant – *tolerant* religion – *Religion;* religious – *religiös* consciousness – *Bewusstsein;* conscious – *bewusst, bei Bewusstsein*

4 a) scientists, cloning, cells b) cells, embryonic, cells c) duplicate, tissues d) breakthrough, biotechnology e) applicable, human, cells, human, beings f) laboratory

5 a) Bones b) transplantation, organ c) lungs d) stomach e) vomit f) genes g) dehydrated h) skin

6 1.e) 2.g) 3.i) 4.c) 5.h) 6.d)

Unit 8: The tourist industry

1 a) survivor b) tourist c) traveller d) hiker e) adventurer f) guide

2 a) volcano b) untouched c) accessible d) peaceful e) to depart f) bin g) infrastructure h) forest i) barrier reef j) alive k) booking

3 (1) travel – *reisen* (2) catalogues – *Kataloge* (3) destination – *Reiseziel* (4) attractive – *attraktiv* (5) faraway – *weit entfernt* (6) overnight – *über Nacht* (7) resort – *Ferienort* (8) sporting – *Sport-* (9) sightseeing – *Besichtigung* (10) fascinating – *faszinierend*

4 a) pesticide (not a gas) b) airline (not a place) c) sightseeing (not an adjective) d) reef (a place without trees) e) preserve (not an adjective)

5 a) Bioreserves, wild b) Springs c) preserve d) carbon footprint e) extraction f) survival

6 corruption – *Korruption, Bestechlichkeit;* corrupt – *korrupt, bestechlich*
economy – *Wirtschaft;* economic – *wirtschaftlich, Wirtschafts-*
budget – *Haushalt, Etat;* budgetary – *Etat-, Budget-, etatmäßig, haushaltsmäßig*
bankruptcy – *Bankrott, Pleite;* bankrupt – *bankrott, pleite*
industry – *Industrie;* industrial – *industriell*
corporation – *Aktiengesellschaft;* corporate – *Firmen-, Unternehmens-*

economic: connected with the economy of a country
economical: spending money in a careful way

7 1.i) 2.e) 3.a) 4.j) 5.h) 6.b) 7.c) 8.k) 9.g) 10.d) 11.f)

8

O	B	N	K	P	A	R	A	G	L	I	D	I	N	G	G	C	M	Y	Z
T	A	O	L	F	C	G	P	R	U	L	N	X	P	A	R	K	O	U	R
J	E	H	Y	L	I	N	Y	W	H	C	T	E	R	T	S	Y	T	Z	E
E	R	T	I	X	Y	I	C	O	O	R	D	I	N	A	T	I	O	N	L
T	O	Q	E	K	P	W	R	A	W	A	T	M	R	N	J	B	R	U	Y
S	B	I	W	L	I	S	U	T	A	C	K	L	E	P	A	Z	B	L	T
K	I	C	Y	N	Y	N	X	P	C	Y	L	N	B	L	Z	R	O	W	S
I	C	T	V	R	X	U	G	N	J	B	R	C	A	W	I	W	A	M	E
I	S	U	Y	E	K	C	O	H	E	C	I	N	G	X	Y	N	T	N	E
N	S	C	I	T	S	A	N	M	Y	G	C	U	C	Y	W	Q	M	O	R
G	B	O	C	V	R	S	T	Z	R	E	M	Z	L	O	M	U	Y	V	F
M	Y	N	G	N	I	C	N	A	D	M	O	O	R	L	L	A	B	Z	E

Unit 9: Globalisation

1 trader – to trade dependence – to depend risk – to risk mixture – to mix manufacturing – to manufacture elimination – to eliminate globalisation – to globalise
origin – original logistics – logistical authenticity – authentic diversity – diverse race – racial foreigner – foreign option – optional

2 standard: b) custom: c) native: a) manufacturing: c) diversity: b) dependence: a)

3 Suggested answers: a) A merchant is a person who trades products in large amounts.
b) A foreigner is a person who comes from another country.
c) A trader is a person who buys and sells products.
d) A manufacturer is a person who produces things (in large quantities).

4 Europe – European Africa – African North America – North American
South America – South American Asia – Asian Australia – Australian

5 a) globalisation; developing; chances b) manufacturing; making money c) logistics
d) diversity e) multicultural mixture f) global; risk; dependent; industrialized
g) foreigners h) trade; guidelines

Unit 10: International politics

1 to represent – to stand for to carry out – to complete to flee – to escape
zone – area to implement – to fulfil aid – help ally – partner to function – to work
operation – action standard – criterion committee – council to permit – to allow

2 hostile ↔ friendly majority ↔ minority direct ↔ indirect veto ↔ approval
supporter ↔ opponent stable ↔ unstable long-term ↔ short-term
constitutional ↔ unconstitutional

3 Suggested answers:
a) A commissioner is a person who acts officially for his or her government.
b) A commander-in-chief is the top leader of the military.
c) A countryman is someone who comes from your country.

4 register – *Liste, Register, Verzeichnis*; to register – *(sich) registrieren, einschreiben, anmelden* delegate – *Delegierte(r), Abgeordnete(r), Bevollmächtigte(r)*; to delegate – *beauftragen, delegieren, bevollmächtigen* limit – *Grenze*; to limit – *begrenzen*
function – *Funktion*; to function – *funktionieren* aid – *Hilfe*; to aid – *helfen*
escape – *Flucht, Entkommen, Ausweg*; to escape – *flüchten (vor)*

5 legislation – *Legislative, Gesetzgebung*; legislative – *gesetzgebend*
judiciary – *Judikative, Justizgewalt, Gerichtswesen*; judicial – *rechtsprechend, gerichtlich*
federation – *Föderation, Bundesstaat*; federal – *Bundes-*
bureaucracy – *Bürokratie*; bureaucratic – *bürokratisch*
tragedy – *Tragödie*; tragic – *tragisch*

6 a) passes b) break c) reverse d) approve e) nominate f) afford g) arrange

7 delegate: b) to persecute: c) illiterate: b) despair: a) hostility: a)

8 1.f) 2.a) 3.d) 4.c) 5.b) 6.e)

9 a) prevent; declarations b) humanitarian c) conditions; slums
d) migrated; persecution e) refuge f) rations

10 peacekeeping mission – *Friedensmission* desperate situation – *verzweifelte Lage* armed forces – *Militär, Streitkräfte* refugee camp – *Flüchtlingslager* non-governmental organization – *Nichtregierungsorganisation* personal belongings – *persönliche Habe* safety zone – *Sicherheitszone* short-term measures – *kurzfristige Maßnahmen*

11 **Across:** 4 orientate 5 disappear 10 concentration 12 treaty 13 executive 14 committee
Down: 1 constitution 2 democracy 3 referendum 6 accession 7 appointment 8 voter 9 bill 11 enlargement

Units 11–14: Cross-cultural communication

1 draft – to draft security – to secure availability – to avail attachment – to attach reference – to refer (to) appreciation – to appreciate reduction – to reduce accomodation – to accomodate identification – to identify response – to respond celebration – to celebrate requirement – to require inquiry – to inquire apology – to apologize bill – to bill queue – to queue stay – to stay caller – to call expiry – to expire request – to require

2 a) appreciate b) attach c) draft d) request e) apologize f) identify g) reduce h) call

3 emotion – emotional politeness – polite inconvenience – inconvenient intensity – intense culture – cultural uniqueness – unique nation – national vacancy – vacant

4 a) vacancy b) unique c) inconvenience d) emotional e) intense

5 a) Pleased/Nice to meet you. b) Take a seat, please. c) What a pity!
d) To make a long story short. e) Sorry for the inconvenience.
f) Please give Mr Wilkinson my regards. g) We'll be in touch.
h) Sorry, I didn't quite catch that. i) All the lines are busy at the moment.
j) Have a nice stay in our town. k) Take care./See you.

6 reservation stay single available floor appreciate floor charge rate security expiry expiry confirmation

7 1.f) 2.d) 3.a) 4.c) 5.g) 6.e) 7.b)

8 1 salutation 2 reference 3 complimentary close 4 thank 5 delighted 6 brackets 7 sincerely
Solution: letters = *1. Briefe, 2. Buchstaben*

9 a) cosmopolitan; overseas b) elevator c) restrooms d) check e) dress code f) shake g) identifiable h) colloquial; conversations; informal i) intense; strangers

Service im Internet

Unter den unten stehenden Freeway Online-Links finden Sie die Vokabeln des Vocabulary Notebook zum Download im MP3-Format, damit Sie die Aussprache hören und üben können.

Außerdem haben Sie die Möglichkeit, unter **800041-0040** die berufsspezifischen Vokabeln zu den Bereichen Wirtschaft, Technik und Sozialwesen sowie unter **800041-0030** den alphabetischen Wortschatz zum Schülerbuch einschließlich des Grundwortschatzes abzurufen.

Gehen Sie einfach auf **www.klett.de** und geben Sie in das Suchfeld den **Online-Link** ein. Der passende Link findet sich immer auf der ersten Seite einer Unit.

Um zur Übersicht aller Materialien zum Lehrwerk zu gelangen, geben Sie bitte **800041-0000** ein.

Unit	Online-Link
Unit 1	800041-0001
Unit 2	800041-0002
Unit 3	800041-0003
Unit 4	800041-0004
Unit 5	800041-0005
Unit 6	800041-0006
Unit 7	800041-0007
Unit 8	800041-0008
Unit 9	800041-0009
Unit 10	800041-0010
Units 11–14	800041-0011

Weitere Angebote	Online-Link
berufsspezifische Vokabeln zu den Bereichen Wirtschaft, Technik und Sozialwesen	800041-0040
alphabetischer Wortschatz aus dem Schülerbuch einschließlich Grundwortschatz (Deutsch – Englisch)	800041-0030
unregelmäßige Verben	800041-0050